The Life and Times of
GEORGE I

The Life and Times of
GEORGE I

Joyce Marlow

Introduction by Antonia Fraser

Book Club Associates, London

*Series design by Paul Watkins
Layout by Andrew Shoolbred*

*Filmset by Keyspools Limited, Golborne, Lancashire
Printed and bound in Great Britain by
Morrison & Gibb Ltd, London & Edinburgh*

Contents

Introduction

THERE IS A CURIOUS FASCINATION about the dour strange personality of our first Hanoverian King, George I. It springs initially from contemplation of the remarkable twists of fate by which this undistinguished ruler of the German state of Hanover came to ascend the British throne. After all, who would have thought in 1660, the year of George's birth, the year also of the Restoration of the monarchy in England, that half a century later this same minor princeling would have replaced the last representative of the romantic House of Stuart as English sovereign? It was true that George was descended via his mother, the lively Electress Sophia, from James I; but it has been calculated that at least fifty-seven cousins actually had a better claim. Yet in 1714, on the death of the childless Queen Anne, it was the Elector George of Hanover who found himself chosen as the representative of the vital Protestant Succession.

So to England at last came the man the Stuart supporters had once scornfully dismissed as 'the wee, wee Germain lairdie', now triumphantly transformed into 'George by the Grace of God, King of Great Britain'. German however the new monarch firmly remained, or perhaps Hanoverian would be a fairer description since to the end of his life he continued to keep the interests of the Electorate firmly to the fore of his attention. Nor did he make any great effort to Anglicise himself, unless the adoption of one English mistress in the latter half of his reign be regarded in that light – even in that sphere, it was more relevant that he had arrived in 1714 with two powerful German mistresses, the ample Madame Kielmansegge and the emaciated Mademoiselle Schulenberg, who continued to dominate the scene. The irreverent English duly nicknamed them the Elephant and the Maypole. In other ways too George's English subjects found plenty to mock in their German-accented King, whose command of English and appreciation of their culture never rose much further than the characteristic remark: 'I hate all boets and bainters.' In his whole thirteen-year reign, George made only one provincial tour. Against this might be put his genuine love of music, his friendship with and patronage of Handel: but Handel of course was another German, although unlike the King he preferred the freedom of the English Court.

Joyce Marlow, in a narrative at once fair-minded and elegantly turned, does not pull her punches where the character

7

of the King is concerned. The vindictive incarceration of his wife, the unfortunate if foolish Sophia Dorothea, is shown not as an aberration but as a foretaste of that malice which he was capable of showing to his relatives when cross, in short a presage of the hideous feuds between Hanoverian fathers and sons. The very real colour of the times, which Joyce Marlow amply demonstrates, lay far more in the society over which this King presided. The great literary flowering of the age of Queen Anne continued: Swift wrote *Gulliver's Travels,* Defoe *Robinson Crusoe.* Above all it was a time of extraordinary political development, not only in terms of Whigs and Tories but the significant rise of Sir Robert Walpole. The South Sea Bubble might swell and burst in a 'delirium of stock-jobbing': nevertheless at the King's death in 1727, the very 'passive solidity', in Joyce Marlow's phrase, with which he had regarded his adopted country, had allowed the emergence of a strong, stable government and a prosperous contented country. It is an ironical truth that many of our sovereigns who have loved us far more, have left us far worse off.

Antonia Fraser

Acknowledgments

Photographs and illustrations were supplied or are reproduced by kind permission of the following. The pictures on pages 42, 68, 71, 79, 100, *122–3*, 196–7, 202, are reproduced by gracious permission of H.M. the Queen; on page *93* by kind permission of the Trustees of Blairs College, Aberdeen; on pages 18, 27, 28–9, 35, by kind permission of the Duke of Brunswick and the Herrenhausen Museum; on pages 118–19 by kind permission of the Duke of Buccleuch and Queensberry; on pages *118–9* from the Castle Howard Collection, Castle Howard, York; on page 192 by kind permission of the Trustees of the Chatsworth Settlement; on pages 84, 206, from the collection of the Marquess of Cholmondeley; on page 129 by courtesy of the Wellcome Trustees; on page 214 from the Gorhambury Collection, by kind permission of the Earl of Verulam; on page 143 from the Saumaraz Collection, Shrubland Park. Bodleian Library, Oxford: 183; Bomann-Museum, Celle: 10–11, *14*, 24, 26; British Federation of Master Printers: 2; British Museum: 36, 48, 62, 64–5, 78, 99, 106–7, 110–11, 121, 124, 132–3, 140–1, 144, 166–7, 168, 170, 171, 179, 188–9, 193, 199, 200–1, 205, 211, 216; Cooper-Bridgman Library: *81*; Heinrich Feesche Verlag: 30–1; Guildhall Library (Su Gooders): *173*; Historisches Museum am Hohen Ufer: *15*, 17, 38–9, 57, 203; A. F. Kersting: 125; London Museum: 112–113, 139; Mansell Collection: 95, 109, 115, 158; Mary Evans Picture Library: 146, 169, 180, 203; National Army Museum: 54–5; National Galleries of Scotland: 88–9, 90, 105; National Monuments Record: 192, 193; National Portrait Gallery: 13, 50, 58, 61, 72, 75, 76, 151, *161*, 161, 164, 171, 174–5, 176; Private Collection: 40, *96*; Royal Academy of Arts: 47, 152–3; Tate Gallery: 79; Victoria and Albert Museum: *3*, 78, *173*, 186; Warburg Institute: 124. Acknowledgments are also due to the photographers, A. C. Cooper Ltd., John Freeman Ltd. and Derrick Witty.

Numbers in italics indicate colour illustrations.

Picture research by Colleen Chesterman.

Map drawn by Design Practitioners Ltd.

1
Life in Hanover
1660-1700

PREVIOUS PAGES Celle, the castle in which Sophia Dorothea grew up and to which she longed to return within weeks of her marriage to the tedious George.

RIGHT Elizabeth of Bohemia, grandmother of George, known as the 'Winter Queen' because of her short reign as Queen of Bohemia.

FOLLOWING PAGES The rise of the Brunswick–Luneberg family: RIGHT an allegorical representation of the Elector Ernest Augustus and his rise to power. LEFT Sophia Dorothea, wife of George, with their two children, George and Sophia Dorothea.

O N 28 MAY 1660, a son was born to Sophia, wife of the Duke of Brunswick-Luneberg or, as he was later more popularly known, the Duke of Hanover. The child was christened George Lewis. Also in May 1660, Charles II of the House of Stuart was restored to the English throne. There was no apparent link between the two events and nobody appears to have prophesied that fifty-four years later, the child born George Lewis of Brunswick-Luneberg would become King of England. It was a sad omission in an era in which astrology was treated so seriously and royal astrologers were so deeply involved with their charts and forecasts. However, it was an understandable omission, as the majority of Englishmen welcomed the Stuart return whole-heartedly. In the years since the execution of Charles I, the inhabitants of England had grown tired of life without a monarch, without ceremony, without glamour, of a life dominated by Oliver Cromwell and the Protectorate, by restrictions and austerity. With the great Cromwell dead, his ineffectual son willingly removed from office, Charles II was restored to the throne, and the legitimate line of the House of Stuart seemed firmly re-established as the rightful monarchs of England. While Hanover was at the time the small duchy of Brunswick-Luneberg, situated in the plains of North Germany, spreading along the valleys of the Weser and Aller, with the town of Hanover as its capital; and the connection with England was minimal.

George Lewis's mother, Sophia, was the daughter of the sad, romantic 'Winter Queen', Elizabeth of Bohemia, who in her turn was the eldest daughter of James I of England. It was thus through Sophia that the claim to the English throne lay, but it seemed remote and unimportant in 1660. Apart from the happily restored Charles II, then in the prime of his life, and his close relatives, there were other grand-children of James I alive, many with better claims than Sophia. In any case, neither Sophia nor her husband was interested in pushing the claim, and the likelihood of her one day being asked to accept the English crown seemed non-existent.

Sophia was an interesting character, and she would have made an excellent Queen of England. She was lively and intelligent – an English visitor to Hanover described her as 'a woman of incomparable knowledge in divinity, philosophy,

12

Queen of Bohemia

13

Sophia, Electress of
Hanover, George's gifted
and vivacious mother,
who so nearly became
Queen of England.

history and the subjects of all sorts of books'. He also reported,
'She speaks five languages so well that by her accent it might be
a dispute which of 'em was her first', the languages being low-
Dutch, German, French, Italian and English. Other commen-
tators intimated that Sophia was not as brilliant and accomplished as she was made out to be. They said that she was turned
into a lady of high intelligence and artistic ability by pro-
Hanoverian writers who had to make at least one member of
the family that had succeeded to the English throne sound
interesting.

While it is true that Sophia was not *the* most gifted of seventeenth-century ladies, and her talents may have been overblown
by her admirers, she was nonetheless an intelligent woman. She
also possessed a shrewd common sense and the fortunate
temperament which can accept the limitations of a situation. It
was as well that her intelligence was matched by an equable
temperament, because her husband, Ernest Augustus, was a
fairly stupid man with no interest whatsoever in the arts or
philosophy.

Ernest Augustus, father of the future George I of England,
was a member of the House of Brunswick and a descendant of
the ancient Guelph family. He was a man of physical courage,
but in addition to a narrow limited mind, he had a cold, reserved
temperament. The main interests of this unenthusiastic man
were horses and women. If Ernest Augustus had no passions in
life, he had one obsession: a determination to strengthen the
position of his duchy, Brunswick-Luneberg.

According to Germanic law, the first-born son did not
inherit all the father's realms. The result over the centuries had
been the splitting of originally large, powerful states into dozens
of small, comparatively powerless ones. In the process, there had
been interminable inter-family fights and feuds. As a contemporary wrote, 'The history of the House of Brunswick is just
like the birthright of Esau and Jacob; the elder brother lets his
blessing be taken by the younger, and then wants to have it back
again.' Ernest Augustus was determined to put a stop to this, at
least as far as Hanover was concerned. He was determined to
rebuild his patrimony into a comparatively powerful state and
to establish the law of primogeniture, whereby his eldest son
would inherit the whole.

16

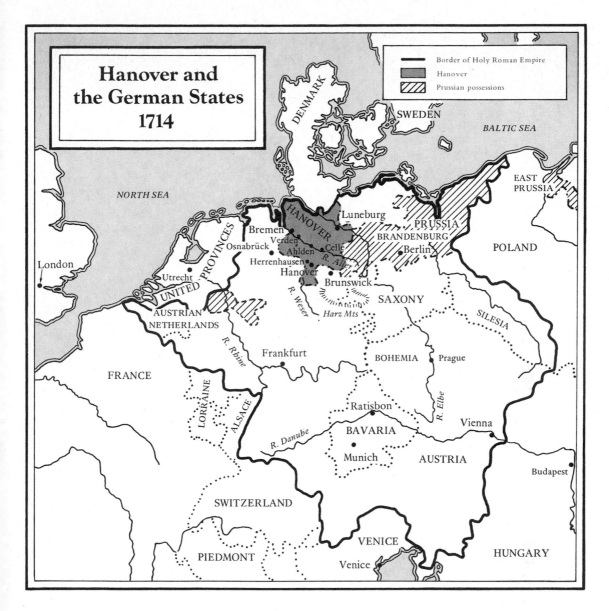

Border of Holy Roman Empire
Hanover
Prussian possessions

DENMARK

SWEDEN

BALTIC SEA

NORTH SEA

EAST
PRUSSIA

HANOVER

Luneburg

PRUSSIA

Bremen

BRANDENBURG

Verden

Celle

Osnabrück

Berlin

POLAND

London

Ahlden

R. Aller

Herrenhausen

Hanover

UNITED PROVINCES

Utrecht

Brunswick

SAXONY

AUSTRIAN
NETHERLANDS

R. Weser

Harz Mts

SILESIA

R. Rhine

FRANCE

Frankfurt

BOHEMIA

Prague

R. Elbe

LORRAINE

ALSACE

Ratisbon

Vienna

R. Danube

BAVARIA

Munich

AUSTRIA

Budapest

SWITZERLAND

VENICE

HUNGARY

PIEDMONT

Venice

The design by which Ernest Augustus hoped to strengthen Hanover's position was twofold. He aimed to have Hanover admitted as the ninth electorate of the Holy Roman Empire, and he further aimed to assimilate the duchy of Kalenberg (which belonged to his brother, the Duke of Celle) with the united territories under his control. The integration of Kalenberg with Brunswick-Luneberg was the more practical scheme, but Hanover's admission as the ninth electorate of the Holy

OPPOSITE
Ernest Augustus, Elector of Hanover, father of George, who ruled Hanover with a benevolent despotism and ensured the absorption of the duchy of Kalenberg into his own territories by the marriage of George to Sophia Dorothea of Celle.

Roman Empire was the project which had the greater appeal for Ernest Augustus. The Holy Roman Empire had been founded by Charlemagne in the ninth century and had long been a powerful force in European politics. But by the end of the seventeenth century, the links with Rome and the Pope had been severed, the days of glory were over and the Empire was a loose association of German states dominated by the Hapsburgs. However, the façade of an empire remained and Hanover's admission as an electorate would enhance its prestige and, in theory if not in practice, its power. (The heads of the states forming the Holy Roman Empire elected their Emperor, hence the terms 'elector' and 'electorate'.)

As the young George Lewis grew up, his father was intent on turning his ambitions into reality. Over the years, Ernest Augustus plotted and schemed, both within his family circle and in the wider sphere of European politics. He persuaded his brother the Duke of Celle not to marry, officially anyway, and to allow Kalenberg to be merged with Brunswick-Luneberg when the Duke died. In the wider field of Europe, he sent Hanoverian troops to support the Holy Roman Empire in its battles with the Turks, and by the time he died, in 1698, he had received some reward for his endeavours. In 1692, Ernest Augustus had been granted the title of Elector – though the full electoral dignity was not conferred until the year after his death, in 1699 – and it was certain that Kalenberg would pass into Hanoverian hands on the Duke of Celle's death. George Lewis accepted his father's ambitions. He believed that the widening and strengthening of Hanover was the duty of its rulers.

George Lewis – and by the two christian names he was always known until 1714, when 'King George Lewis of England' would not have done, and the second name was dropped – was his father's son. It is difficult to believe that the shrewd, intelligent Sophia, with her lively interest in the arts and philosophy, actually bore him. He inherited none of her qualities, except perhaps her sense of knowing when *not* to interfere politically. The only trait he appears to have gained from her was a love of walking. Sophia was described as 'the most constant and greatest walker'. George Lewis also enjoyed tramping round the gardens of his palaces for hours on end, first in Hanover, later in London, exhausting his courtiers in the process. He certainly did not inherit Sophia's flair for languages, as he was to prove in England, nor her interest in cultural matters, as he proved all his life.

Physically he was a Guelph, with the bulbous eyes and sallow complexion characteristic of that dynasty. He was described by an unsympathetic observer as being 'low of stature, of features coarse, of aspect dull and placid', also Guelph characteristics. A more friendly observer wrote, 'He's a proper, middle-sized, well proportioned man, of gentle address and good appearance', but even this pro-Hanoverian writer admitted, 'He's not much addicted to any diversions besides hunting.' Mentally, too, George Lewis was his father's son. He had the same limited interests, horses – and women. He had the same narrow mind that could grasp nothing other than the Hanoverian cause. He inherited the hearty Guelph appetite – consuming vast quantities of food was a major pre-occupation. But he was even more reserved than his father, a genuinely shy man who hated large gatherings or the splendid occasion where he was the centre of attention. His shyness, allied to the limited intellect, also made him a suspicious man. He was happy only in the company of people he had known for years, whom he had grown to trust. He preferred listening 'to the labour of talking himself', but he needed to listen to people who, while not overtaxing his brain, would give him due deference. Despite his shyness and hatred of ceremony, he was the ruler of Hanover.

And Hanover was a despotic state. Absolute power lay with the Elector. There was a Prime Minister, a Foreign Minister, a Chief Treasurer and other ministers. The various local territories that Hanover had already absorbed – and was to continue to absorb – had their *landtags* or legislative assemblies which were supposed to be autonomous. But in practice, every decision, whether concerning home or foreign affairs, whether of major or minor importance, had to be referred to the Elector. All expenditure above the sum of fifty thalers (approximately £12) had to be sanctioned by him, any major criminal prosecution had to be instituted by him, and ministers were appointed and dismissed by him. He was also commander-in-chief of the army, which was in effect his personal property. Hanoverian troops were sent to support or loaned to other European rulers at the will of the Elector.

'Low of stature, of features coarse, of aspect dull and placid'

However, in practice it was a benevolent despotism. Paternally, the Elector Ernest Augustus, followed by his son George Lewis, ordered the lives of his subjects. Hanover was a reasonably prosperous country, possessed of rich farming land, with a flourishing woollen and linen trade. It also tapped the mineral resources of the Hartz mountains – an observer wrote, 'His Highness draws a mighty profit from his silver mines in the Hartz.' As there was not too much poverty, as there had never been a tradition of political dissent or a semblance of Parliamentary government, the Elector's subjects were content to have their lives thus ordered from above. After George Lewis had become Elector, it was said, 'his administration is most equitable, mild and prudent. He's the most beloved by his subjects of any Prince in the World. There is no division or faction among them, by reason of his impartial favour.'

'His administration is most equitable, mild and prudent'

It was a far cry from England, where there was a great deal of division and faction, where there was an extremely noisy Parliament which did not believe that its monarchs had the unquestioned and unquestionable right to rule. But in the 1680s and early 1690s, the shy, suspicious, sluggish-minded young man who was to become King of England, who was to move abruptly from the neat, well-ordered despotic state of Hanover to the sprawling complexities of English politics, had little interest in what was occurring in that rowdy island.

In the year of 1680, George Lewis had visited England for the first time. The idea behind the visit was the possibility of his marrying the Princess Anne, and thus strengthening the Hanoverian position by an alliance with England. After nearly two decades on the throne, Charles II remained childless. His heir-presumptive was his brother, James, and the suitable marriage of James's younger daughter by his first wife was therefore of some importance. However, in 1680 it did not appear to be overwhelmingly important: James had re-married, and the probability of his second wife producing a son – which indeed she did – was high. In the event, George Lewis did not care for Anne, nor she for him. But more vital than their mutual feelings was the fact that political negotiations on the marriage started to founder, and Ernest Augustus called his son home. That Ernest Augustus recalled George Lewis so abruptly is an indication of the minimal interest the House of

Hanover had in an English connection or in English affairs. For, though both father and son were obsessively eager to solidify their state, and were not in the least averse to swallowing up the minnows on their borders, they had no vast territorial ambitions, no great power lust. This was as well, because they had neither the intelligence nor the energy to turn Hanover into a great power. Both were content, and mentally equipped, to have and to hold in a limited field.

Back in Hanover in the early 1680s, the father and son concentrated on the limited field. In 1682, Ernest Augustus decided that the most useful marriage for his heir would be that with Sophia Dorothea (who is not to be confused with George Lewis's mother, Sophia). Sophia Dorothea was George Lewis's cousin, the daughter of the Duke of Celle by his morganatic union with a Frenchwoman. Thus, in effect, by arranging this marriage, Ernest Augustus took out an extra insurance policy to guarantee Kalenberg's passing into Hanoverian hands when the Duke died. It was an insurance of which George Lewis strongly approved.

If royal weddings were dictated by political issues and power struggles, sometimes they worked out happily and successfully, but not so in the case of George Lewis and Sophia Dorothea. The first child, the future George II, was born in 1683 within a year of the marriage, but the second child, the future wife of Frederick William of Prussia, was not born until 1688 and there were no miscarriages or still-births in between. In furtherance of Hanoverian ambitions, George Lewis was away at the wars during this period, fighting for the Emperor against the Turks. He displayed particular bravery at the relief of Vienna. But the time lapse between the births indicates how poor the relationship with his wife was, because George Lewis was not permanently absent for five years. He did return to Hanover from time to time. On one occasion, he brought with him, as part of the spoils of the Turkish campaign, two Muslim servants, Mustapha and Mahomet. They were later to cause much comment in England, and to be painted into a fresco at Kensington Palace.

In truth, George Lewis and Sophia Dorothea disliked each other from their first meeting, and within a short while the dislike had grown into loathing. She had many of her mother-in-law's qualities, being lively, ardent and intelligent, with an

Sophia Dorothea, the headstrong young wife of George, lively but lacking the shrewdness and intelligence of her mother-in-law. Her indiscreet flaunting of her relationship with Count Königsmark led to her lifelong imprisonment and separation from her children.

extra *joie de vivre* inherited from her French mother. Unfortunately, the elder Sophia's interest in the arts had not led her to create an artistic circle in the food-and-horse-dominated Hanoverian Court, a circle such as Sophia Dorothea could have joined or extended. Even more unfortunately, Sophia Dorothea possessed neither her mother-in-law's common sense nor her ability to come to terms with a situation. Sophia Dorothea was head-strong and filled with youthful certainty. She wanted to mould life to her shape, to have it on her terms. Being married to a dull young man whom she actively disliked was not the shape she envisaged.

At the time of the marriage, George Lewis already had one official mistress, and he was to acquire more. Going to bed on the odd occasion with the ruler was not sufficient to turn a woman into an official mistress, the relationship had to be further defined until it was recognised that Madame X was the king or elector's mistress, and she then received the deference due to her status. If there were several ladies who acquired the status, the one who emerged on top, metaphorically speaking, was known as the *maîtresse en titre*, or chief mistress. When Sophia Dorothea learned that George Lewis had an official mistress, instead of calmly accepting the not unusual situation as her mother-in-law had earlier done with Ernest Augustus, she created a scene and said she wanted to go home to Celle. This she obviously could not do, and her reaction was probably caused as much by sheer boredom with life at the Hanoverian Court and the desire to be free of George Lewis as by his actual infidelity. Within a few years, life was to cease to be boring for Sophia Dorothea, because in 1689 Count Philip von Königs-mark was appointed a Colonel of Dragoons at the Court.

Königsmark came from a Swedish family that was both illustrious and notorious. His sister was the mistress of the King of Poland, and a brother had been involved in the murder of an Englishman but had bribed the jury and managed to escape retribution. Königsmark was part mercenary soldier, part knight errant, by no means an attractive character, though he was physically handsome. From the moment of his arrival in Hanover, he courted Sophia Dorothea assiduously, initially with the instincts of a professional lover, though it seems prob-able that by the end of the relationship he genuinely cared for her. She in her turn, bored, restless, unhappy and still very young – she was only sixteen when she married George Lewis – responded to the flattery and attention. Within a few years, it was widely believed that they were lovers. This of itself would not necessarily have caused trouble but unfortunately both Sophia Dorothea and Königsmark flaunted their relationship. They failed to pay attention to the repeated warnings of Ernest Augustus and the shrewd Sophia to be more discreet. Whatever the true nature of their relationship – and many believed that she was not actually his mistress, but merely a young woman enamoured of the idea of love – by 1694, Königsmark's drunken

Count Philip von Königsmark, the attractive soldier who captured the heart of Sophia Dorothea, and whose disappearance was never fully accounted for.

boastings in the taverns of far too many German towns, and Sophia Dorothea's romantic posturings at Court, had become too much for Ernest Augustus or his son to bear. The family name and honour was being dragged into ridicule and disrepute. And Sophia Dorothea had fulfilled her function, which was to produce an heir.

On 1 July 1694, Königsmark was definitely seen to enter the apartment of Sophia Dorothea – who was not present – and equally definitely never again seen alive. In December of the same year, Sophia Dorothea was tried at the Consistorial Court of Hanover and Celle, and divorced by George Lewis. According to the terms of the divorce, she was forbidden to re-marry or ever again to see her children. She was then twenty-eight years old, and shortly afterwards she was taken to the castle of Ahlden where she spent the rest of her life. One slight attempt at reconciliation was supposedly made by George Lewis to which Sophia Dorothea supposedly replied, with considerable dignity,

The Countess von Platen, *maîtresse en titre* of the Elector Ernest Augustus, nicknamed *'die Böse'* for her supposed complicity in the Königsmark affair.

'Tell the Prince he requires an impossibility – for if I am guilty, I am unworthy of him, and if I am innocent, he is unworthy of me.'

One says 'supposedly', because from the moment Königsmark disappeared, the rumours and attributed statements started to proliferate like weeds in an untended garden. The Courts, and the ordinary citizens, of Europe had a scandal of the first magnitude to discuss. And discuss it they did. The most widely held belief was that Königsmark had been murdered in Sophia Dorothea's apartment, his body hacked to pieces and buried beneath the floorboards. (And years later, in the time of George II, his remains were said to have been dug up during renovations to the palace.) One set of the proliferating rumours stated that Ernest Augustus had ordered the assassination with the agreement of his son. Another set had Ernest Augustus actually present in Sophia Dorothea's apartment during the gruesome murder, though it was agreed that George Lewis was

27

not in Hanover when it took place. Their reasons for deciding to dispose of Königsmark were said to be that positive proof in the shape of intercepted letters had come into their hands: proof that Sophia Dorothea intended to elope with Königsmark that very night – an event that could not be allowed to occur. Other rumours had Ernest Augustus's *maîtresse en titre*, the Countess von Platen, as the villain of the piece – and her nickname was '*die Böse*', 'the wicked'. She was supposed to have lured Königs-mark to the apartment with a false message and to have had him killed, either because she was jealous of Sophia Dorothea or because he had spurned her daughter. The saddest set of rumours said that Sophia Dorothea and Königsmark had finally realised

The castle at Ahlden, where George banished his wife Sophia Dorothea for life after her presumed affair with Königsmark.

that their love was star-crossed and could not continue. He had come to the palace to bid the final 'adieu' to his beloved mistress, only to be cruelly butchered, either at the instigation of Ernest Augustus with the connivance of George Lewis, or by the hirelings of the Countess von Platen.

One thing was not in doubt, that Königsmark had been murdered. Another thing became increasingly obvious, that George Lewis was treating the woman to whom he had been married for twelve years and who had borne him two children, with particular unpleasantness. Sophia Dorothea was not physically maltreated at Ahlden castle, but she was allowed neither to leave the grounds nor to receive visitors. Her crime was that of having been a self-willed, high-spirited, romantic young woman married to a boring young man. There was no suggestion of political motivation or plotting in her liaison with Königsmark. Admittedly, as a royal princess, she should have known better than to act so dramatically in the relationship with her Swedish chevalier. But, after a time, George Lewis could have allowed her to see her children. He could have allowed her to receive visitors to enliven the dreary, dragging years. He could eventually have allowed her to return home to Celle, which was what she wanted to do (although her father, the Duke, failed to come to her assistance during the divorce proceedings, considering that she had dragged the family name into disrepute and therefore warranted her punishment). Despite the fact that Sophia Dorothea presented no political threat to him, that she had been his wife, George Lewis granted no concessions during the thirty-odd years of her imprisonment at Ahlden. As decade followed decade, he acted towards her with continuing cold, insensitive malice. Thereby he revealed a marked attribute of his otherwise passive, placid character – a callous vindictiveness towards close relatives who attempted to thwart him. There was the family history of internecine warfare, and Horace Walpole later said that it came from 'something in the blood'. It was a 'something' which George Lewis inherited in a particularly virulent form, as his relationship with his only son was further to demonstrate.

As a result of the mystery surrounding Königsmark's murder and the manner in which George Lewis treated his wife, the affair remained a favourite scandal for years. Secret histories,

Herrenhausen, Home of the Hanoverian Dynasty

The Hanoverian Court established itself at
Herrenhausen, a country house just outside Hanover,
in 1666. The house and gardens were transformed
between 1696 and 1710 by the Electress Sophia
who was responsible for restyling and enlarging the
entire gardens. She often wrote: 'The garden is my
very life.'

BELOW A panorama of the gardens, showing the
900-yard-long rectangle which forms the Gross
Garten, which was surrounded by a moat and
comprised French pleasure gardens, fountains,
open-air theatres, a maze and the much admired
orangeries.

ABOVE The Great Gallery of the Herrenhausen Palace, with murals by Giusti.

LEFT A large urn in the garden, with the house in the background.

intimate revelations, 'the true story of …' flooded the market, and the legend of the sad prisoner of Ahlden continued to capture the imagination of Europe.

If George Lewis's behaviour towards Sophia Dorothea did his personal reputation little good, it in no way affected his political position or Hanoverian life in general. This life, which Sophia Dorothea had found so appallingly dull, centred on the Court at Herrenhausen which was 'an English mile and a half from Hanover'. The foundations of the palace had been laid in 1665, and like so many European palaces of the time, whether or not their rulers gave allegiance to France, it had been modelled on Versailles. Over the years, Herrenhausen had been enlarged, notably by Ernest Augustus. By 1700, it possessed a vast moat on which gondolas floated – an English visitor noted that 'the water works' were 'great and noble'. It had intricate formal gardens with busts of twenty-three Roman emperors especially imported from Paris, in this instance by George Lewis. It had acres of informal parkland, as the English visitor again noted, 'curiously contrived and decked with perpetual verdure'. There were stables for over six hundred horses, which in view of the Hanoverian proclivity for hunting was not surprising. There was also an open-air theatre which was 'perfect … excellently cut into green seats, the dressing rooms for the actors being so many bowers and summer houses on each side'. The particular feature of Herrenhausen on which all visitors commented was the orangeries. That great letter-writer, lady of the Court, wit and blue-stocking, Lady Mary Wortley Montagu recorded: 'I was particularly impressed at the vast number of orange trees, much larger than I have ever seen in England, although the climate is certainly colder.' Lady Mary was also impressed by the Hanoverian heating arrangements which assisted the growth of the oranges and which she considered could be usefully imported into the warmer, if hardly tropical, English climate.

The English visitor from whose observations we have already quoted was John Toland. He was a noted Dissenting minister, biographer of John Milton, translator of Aesop's fables and pro-Hanoverian. He travelled through the electorate soon after George Lewis became its ruler. He described the Court as 'extremely polite and, even in Germany, it is accounted the best

'I was particularly impressed at the vast number of orange trees'

both for Civility and Decorum'. He also wrote, 'I never knew a greater Sobriety, or a more exact Government in a private family.' The emphasis was on decorum and sobriety, which was by some translated as dullness. Sophia Dorothea was not alone in considering Herrenhausen a stolidly boring palace, an imitation of Versailles in structural detail only, not in the quality of life. As already indicated, even the elder Sophia failed to give it glamour or glitter or a true intellectual content.

Sophia, however, had one notable association, and that was with the philosopher and mathematician Gottfried Wilhelm Leibnitz. Through Sophia's good offices, Leibnitz was appointed librarian at Hanover in 1676, and the Electress and the philosopher forged a deep friendship. Leibnitz was the man responsible for the immortal dictum 'All is for the best in the best of all possible worlds', later to be so savagely satirised by Voltaire in *Candide*. He coined this surprising dictum, which made so many writers other than Voltaire gnash their teeth with rage, in a philosophical/theological work entitled *Théodicé*. It was an analysis of good and evil and a defence of optimism, a more profound work than the celebrated dictum might indicate. Leibnitz was a man of high talent, a mathematician who produced fundamental work on differential calculus, a philosopher of renown. His company gave Sophia great solace and pleasure.

While Sophia satisfied her mind, her son George Lewis satisfied his body. In considering 'the exact government' of family life at Herrenhausen, an observer such as John Toland had to overlook the fact that George Lewis's wife was divorced and imprisoned in Ahlden castle, and that his mistresses reigned supreme. By 1700, there were several of them, and the relationship of George Lewis's mistresses, to him and to each other, is confusing. If one judges by contemporary references, the entire von Platen family, on the female side, seems to have served the electors, father and son. However, there were only two ladies who accompanied George Lewis to London: one was Madame Kielmansegge, and everybody agreed that she was the daughter of the elder Countess von Platen, Ernest Augustus's *maîtresse en titre*. A later defender of George Lewis's reputation, while concurring that Madame Kielsmansegge was the Countess von Platen's daughter, emphatically stated she was the child of Ernest Augustus, not of the Countess's titular husband. Therefore she was George Lewis's half-sister and the relationship was strictly platonic. This was not a view held by contemporaries. They were equally emphatic that the relationship was that of lover and mistress (and they did not mention the possibility of Madame Kielmansegge being Ernest Augustus's child). John Toland, without actually mentioning the word 'mistresses', picked out the relevant ladies for pen-portraits. He wrote, 'Madame de Kielmansegge, daughter of the Count of Platen, may pass for a woman of sense and wit.' On the whole, contemporaries agreed that Madame Kielmansegge had some intelligence and animation. It was noted that she actually liked reading, although what sort of books she enjoyed was not recorded.

Madame Kielmansegge's wit and animation was relative to the lady who was George Lewis's *maîtresse en titre*. She was Ehrengard Melusina von der Schulenberg, commonly referred to as Mademoiselle Schulenberg. She was not a member of the von Platen family, but was one of the Electress Sophia's ladies-in-waiting. About Mademoiselle Schulenberg few had any kind words to say. Even the enthusiastic John Toland had to be content with the brief statement that she was 'a lady of extraordinary merit', while the Electress Sophia said, 'Do you see that mawkin? You would scarcely believe that she has captivated my son.' Mademoiselle Schulenberg was tall and thin, both intensely superstitious and deeply religious. It was said that she went to the Lutheran chapel seven times on Sundays. Of character, she was placid and passive – the only thing that brought her to life was the scent of money – and her brain power was equally sluggish. But she suited George Lewis, who did not care for lively or intelligent women and, after his fashion, he was faithful to her. Neither Madame Kielmansegge nor Mademoiselle Schulenberg was regarded as an adornment to anybody's household, but both ladies were to wield great power when their royal lover became King of England.

As the eighteenth century dawned, the Elector of Hanover was not 'the wee, wee German lairdie', so contemptuously described by Stuart supporters. Apart from its electors' ambitions and their success in realising them, geographically Hanover's position made it of some importance in the spectrum of European politics and battles for power. Hanover lay close

Madame Sophia von Kielmansegge, daughter of the Countess von Platen. She accompanied George to England, where she acquired the title of Countess of Darlington.

Ehrengard Melusina von der Schulenberg, George's *maîtresse en titre*, painted as a young girl. She later became Duchess of Kendal and George spent much of his leisure time at her villa at Isleworth.

to what for so long had been the cockpit of Europe, the Low Countries (by 1700 the United Provinces, dominated by Holland). It bordered on Brandenberg/Prussia and it had access to the Baltic Sea. Thus Hanover's allegiance had been and was to continue to be of interest to the major European powers. Its proximity to the United Provinces made anybody contemplating attacking them need Hanoverian support; its bordering Brandenberg/Prussia, which was already showing signs of a greater power complex, again made Hanoverian support useful for those wishing to dampen that complex, while the access to the Baltic meant that Hanover was of strategic importance in containing the Northern powers of Sweden and Denmark and the yet unknown ambitions of that vast country then on the hinterlands of Europe, Russia.

In practice, because of its despotic rule and relative stability, Hanover had been consistent in its alliances, more so than most small – or for that matter large – European states. Its natural allegiance went to the Holy Roman Empire, and the dominant Hapsburgs in Vienna. But Hanover had also been 'most hearty in the common cause of Europe', that common cause being fear and distrust of Louis XIV's France and a determination to curtail its power. Apart from supporting the Holy Roman Empire in its Turkish wars, Ernest Augustus had also sent Hanoverian troops to fight in the Wars of the League of Augsburg. Under George Lewis, Hanover was to continue to support the European countries ranged against France in the next war to erupt, in 1701. Like his father, he was to continue to expect due pickings for Hanover.

In 1700, an event occurred in England which was to transform the Hanoverian destiny, to put the electors into a position in which they could have pickings beyond their wildest dreams. In 1700, the Duke of Gloucester died: he was the sole remaining child of the innumerable pregnancies of the, by now heir to the English throne, the same Princess Anne whom George Lewis had failed to marry in 1680. The boy's death made it essential that an heir to succeed Anne be legally proclaimed. There was only one descendant of the House of Stuart who fulfilled the requirements of the reigning King of England. That descendant was George Lewis's mother, the grand-daughter of James I.

THE GLORIOUS BATTLE
of BLENHEIM
August the 13. 1704.

2
The Waiting Game 1701-13

I N 1700, THE REIGNING ENGLISH MONARCH was the childless, Dutch-born William III. He had struck out for the throne and obtained it with the backing of Parliament in the 'Glorious Revolution' of 1688 – 'Glorious' because the deposing of the Catholic, Stuart, James II and the enthronement of the Protestant, Orange, William had been achieved with the minimum of bloodshed and the maximum benefit to Parliament. William's claim to the throne rested on the fact that his wife, Mary, was the elder daughter of James II's first, Protestant marriage. Officially, he only shared it with Mary, at least until her death in 1694. William wanted the throne so that he could ally England with Holland against the power of Louis XIV's France. The safety of Holland and the belief that French dominance must be curtailed were the mainsprings of William's life.

The Princess Anne was, as the younger daughter of James II's first marriage, the next undisputed heir. But when her last surviving son died in 1700, William was determined not only to ensure a Protestant Succession after her, but that it should be the Hanoverian one. It was computed that there were fifty-seven descendants of James I who had a better claim to the throne than the Electress Sophia, and some of them were Protestants, too. But Hanover had the vital qualification for William III – the electorate had proved itself most hearty in the common cause of Europe against Louis XIV. Even if the exiled Catholic Stuarts decided to reverse Henri of Navarre's judgment that 'Paris is worth a Mass' into 'The English throne is worth *not* saying a Mass', William still did not want them to succeed. The Stuart place of exile was France. A Stuart king might make an alliance with France as Charles II had done. The long-fought battles to contain France could be negated and the safety and sovereignty of William's beloved Holland might again be threatened.

There remained in England considerable sympathy for the Stuart claims to the throne, partly nostalgic, partly based on guilt feelings and partly on legitimacy. Anne's claim was legitimate as the Stuart daughter of the deposed James II. But if she died childless, as now seemed most likely, should not the throne revert to the son of James's second marriage? However, apart from that of the most ardent Jacobites, this Stuart support rested on the hope or belief that the possible James III – other-

PREVIOUS PAGES The battle of Blenheim, one of Marlborough's greatest victories, and the first great French defeat since Louis XIV became king.

OPPOSITE William of Orange, probably painted after the victory at the Boyne, who died unmourned by the English.

41

Queen Anne, whose sad
failure to produce a
surviving heir led to
George's accession to the
English throne.

wise James Francis Edward, known to history as 'the Old
Pretender' – would become a Protestant. There were few
people in England who wanted a Catholic on their throne
again. In any case, one of the main clauses of the Bill of Rights
which Parliament had obtained after the 'Glorious Revolution'
was that no Catholic could wear the crown of England. In 1700,
James Francis Edward was not showing any signs of recanting
his Catholicism and entering the Protestant fold. Consequently,
this time – he had tried earlier – William persuaded Parliament
to agree to the Hanoverian Succession.

Thus, in 1701, the Act of Settlement was passed through
Parliament whereby it was decreed 'that the most excellent

Princess Sophia, Electress and Dowager Duchess of Hanover, daughter of Elizabeth, late Queen of Bohemia, daughter of James I, shall be next in succession to the crown'. This was of course assuming, as everyone did, that the unfortunate Anne, who had already produced so many still-born or short-lived infants, would have no further children. But William had to pay dearly for his Hanoverian Succession. Parliament had become increasingly displeased with the behaviour of its Dutch monarch over the last few years. If he wanted the Hanoverian Succession – which Parliament had no objections to either – he would have to make considerable concessions. William, faced by an adamant Parliament, had no choice but to agree to the demands.

These demands, eight in all, were considerable. In the future, when the Hanoverians succeeded to the throne, England would not again go to war in the defence of a foreign country without the consent of Parliament. This clause was deliberately aimed at William who, in 1689, on his own initiative, had taken England into the War of the League of Augsburg which had then become the War of the Grand Alliance. Further, the monarch could not in future leave England without the consent of Parliament, and no foreigner could sit on the Privy Council or hold office under the Crown. These clauses were also aimed at William, who had left England for Holland or elsewhere as he saw fit, and had packed high offices with his Dutch advisers. Some of the other clauses against what a disgruntled Parliament regarded as William's disregard for it, were repealed in 1705. But two further clauses were of abiding importance: the King could no longer dismiss judges, nor could he protect his favourites from impeachment by the Commons or Lords. The former clause was another step towards the independence of the English judiciary, while the latter limited the individual actions of the monarch and his close advisers.

The Act of Settlement was important as a document in the history of the English Parliament, for the future government of the country and, in the long-run, to the well-being of its citizens. It was in effect the culmination of the prolonged battle between Parliament and the Crown. It proved that in the last analysis power now lay with Parliament. What had finally been broken was the 'Divine Right of Kings'; James I's fervent belief

43

that 'Kings are not only called God's lieutenants but even by God himself are called gods'; or his son Charles I's even more fervent belief that 'Parliaments are altogether in my power, for their calling, sitting and dissolutions.'

By its recent actions and demands Parliament had shown that it was no longer at any monarch's beck or call. It had also proved its power in another way. The Hanoverian Successors, the future rulers of England, had been ordained not by the grace of God, nor even by the grace of the King, but by the grace of Parliament. However, the effects of the Act of Settlement were long-term. After it had become law, the King was still expected to rule, and England was far from being a democracy in any real sense of the word, meaning that the majority of her citizens had any say in the governing of their country. On the contrary, when a petition was submitted at this time to Parliament, asking 'that this House will have regard to the Voice of the People', the citizens thus acting as *vox populi* were promptly clapped into gaol for their impertinence.

There are those who have said that what the Act of Settlement really represented was the chauvinistic, isolationist petulance of the Members of Parliament (mostly Tory at the time) determined to show the upstart, foreign William that they could wield a big stick if he did not behave himself. Then there are those who have said that all the Act did was to substitute the despotism of Parliament, drawn from a very limited section of the community, for the despotism of the King. But whatever the motives of the Members of Parliament who made the demands that culminated in the Act of Settlement (and they were in a churlish mood), these further checks on royal power helped England on the road – even if it was a long, winding, uphill road – towards Parliamentary democracy and political maturity.

In 1701, George Lewis showed little interest in the proceedings of this noisy, demanding, self-righteous English Parliament. His lack of interest was understandable. Admittedly, the Act of Settlement stated that the Electress Sophia *and her heirs* should be next in succession to the English throne, and he was the eldest son of the Electress Sophia. But William III was still alive. His heir-presumptive, Anne, was only thirty-six years old (though after her innumerable pregnancies she looked and

44

acted as if she were years older). Then there was his mother Sophia, the designated successor. True she was old, but she showed no signs of diminishing vitality. The enthusiastic John Toland recorded in 1702, when Sophia was already into her seventies, 'She has ever enjoyed extraordinary health ... has not one wrinkle on her face, nor one tooth out of her head, and reads without spectacles.' So why, in 1701, should George Lewis trouble himself about an event which might – or given the fluctuating condition of European politics, might not – happen in the distant future?

Nonetheless, the Earl of Macclesfield and his entourage who brought over to Hanover the document enshrining the succession, were received with due ceremony. Again according to John Toland, 'one of the largest houses in the whole city was assigned for his entertainment. ... The Elector's own servants waited on them every morning with a silver coffee and teapots in their own chambers. Burgundy, champagne, Rhenish and all manner of wines were as common as beer. ... They were entertained with music, balls and plays.' Having fulfilled his duties as a host, George Lewis returned his attention to Hanoverian affairs. It was towards his own country that his duty lay, and on which his limited enthusiasm remained focussed.

'The Elector's own servants waited on them every morning'

Fortunately, Hanover's interests coincided with the English design so there was no clash. This design was basically William III's, his last great effort to check the power of France. The War of the Grand Alliance had ended without decisive results for either the French or the allies. William could see that the power of France threatened to be vastly increased in the near future. The threat this time came from the succession not to the English but to the Spanish throne, for the King of Spain, who was known as Charles the Sufferer, was obviously near death. At the recent treaties ending the War of the Grand Alliance, Louis XIV had agreed not to link the Spanish throne with the French. But when Charles the Sufferer actually died in 1700 he willed his crown to a French Bourbon prince. Louis immediately changed his mind about the treaty, hoping that the English and Dutch were sufficiently war-weary not to baulk him.

The English Parliament was indeed extremely tired of war and against the idea of further involvement on the Continent. But William possessed an iron will and a certainty that French

power must be checked. Before his death, William, and the
Duke of Marlborough who shared his views, managed to
negotiate a further Grand Alliance between England, Holland
and the Holy Roman Empire which committed them to a war
against France. Fortunately for William in his relationship with
an angry Parliament, Louis xiv then made a fatal error. Louis
had earlier recognised William's right to the English crown (as
opposed to the deposed James ii's), but when James ii died in
the autumn of 1701, Louis promptly recognised his son, James
Francis Edward, as the rightful King of England. By this action,
he ensured England's whole-hearted commitment to the Grand
Alliance and to the prosecution of the War of the Spanish
Succession. No French monarch was going to tell England who
her rightful King was or to negate the Act of Settlement as
passed by Parliament.

William iii died in 1702 unmourned by the English. Unkind
toasts were drunk to 'the little gentleman in black velvet', the
little gentleman being the mole who had built the molehill over
which William's horse had stumbled, throwing him badly and
occasioning his death. In effect, though his heart lay in Holland,
William had served England well. He was right in believing
that French power must be broken if Holland – and England –
were to flourish. In practice, it was England not Holland which
benefited most as a result of William's strategy. The War of the
Spanish Succession finally overtaxed Holland's resources, her
years of amazing vitality were ebbing away and the eighteenth
century was to be the century of Europe's largest off-shore
island, soon to be the 'United Kingdom of Great Britain'.
British dominance was to lie in commerce and overseas trade,
and a powerful France controlling the seas would have doomed
her expansion.

George Lewis, the next foreign king whose heart lay in
another country but who also, if for different reasons, served
England well, joined Hanover to the Grand Alliance. The
tortuous course of the War of the Spanish Succession, the aims
that changed, the alliances that were formed and broken, is not
within our scope. It has been charted by Winston Churchill
(among others) in the life of his famous ancestor, the Duke of
Marlborough. He was one of England's greatest generals,
perhaps one of her great statesmen, too, because a leader of a

combined force such as the Grand Alliance required a mastery of strategy and tactics as great off the battlefield as on, if he was to keep the forces combined, the fragile unity intact, amidst the jealousies and personal aims of the European rulers involved, not to mention the jealousies at home.

It was towards the end of 1705 that Marlborough came into serious contact with George Lewis. This was basically in his role of statesman, the political pourer of oil on troubled waters. Earlier in the year, at home in England, the Tories who were out of office had engaged in what they considered to be a clever political manœuvre. The Whigs currently in office were supposedly the opponents of the divine right of kings, the supporters of the power of Parliament and the Hanoverian Succession. Therefore the Tories decided to bring forward a proposal that the Electress Sophia should take up residence in England. They knew this would infuriate Queen Anne who had no liking for her Hanoverian relatives, and suffered from a guilt-complex about the dethronement of her father, James II. They hoped to trip up the Whigs and perhaps cause their downfall. In fact, the latter rushed to deny Sophia's right to live in England while Anne was alive, and thereby gained more support from the Queen than they had ever had.

A broadside published against the idea of a 'Popish' successor to the English throne – a possibility averted by the Hanoverian connection.

48

In Hanover, the news that the Whigs who were supposed to favour the succession of Sophia were furiously attacking merely a proposal that she live in England, was received with astonishment and perturbation. Did the Whigs want the Hanoverian Succession or did they not? Did they, as the ruling power in England, want Hanoverian support for the war or did they not? Marlborough hastened to Hanover to explain that they did. He arrived as the victor of Blenheim, the most complete defeat of the French forces to date, the battle which, as Winston Churchill wrote, 'changed the political axis of the world'. With his personal charisma, his immense authority, Marlborough had little difficulty in convincing Sophia and George Lewis that the Whigs were their friends and most stalwart in their desire for the Hanoverian Succession.

He was also able to explain the details of the Regency Bill (which became law the next year). This Bill had arisen partly because Anne's health was causing alarm, and it was partly to counteract the Tory manœuvres over Sophia's residence. By its terms a regency consisting of high officers of state and other ministers previously appointed by Hanover would come into being immediately on the death of the Queen. It would rule the country until the Hanoverian successor arrived in England. Thereby any hiatus, any dangerous period without proper leadership, would be bridged, and the possibility of revolution in favour of the Stuarts would be lessened. Also as a result of the Act, the Electress Sophia, George Lewis and his son George (by now in his twenties) became naturalised English citizens. Sophia and George Lewis could not wholly understand why they had to become naturalised like any common-or-garden foreigners, but Marlborough explained that it was due to the peculiar English laws, and that the whole Act would strengthen the hand of those truly desiring a peaceful Hanoverian Succession, notably the Whigs. Mother and son accepted these explanations – though Sophia then tended more towards the Tories. Marlborough departed from Hanover with a splendid gift of a coach and six horses, secure in the knowledge that the designated heirs to the English throne remained contented and that Hanoverian support would be forthcoming for the war.

Both Sophia and George Lewis showed sound judgment in respect of the English political scene, although in the case of

George Lewis, certainly in the middle years of waiting, the reaction continued to be caused more by lack of interest than by judgment. He and his mother studiously refrained from becoming involved in the increasingly bitter entanglements of English politics. They refused to commit themselves to any suggestions made by English politicians, other than such concrete measures as the Regency Act, once they had been fully explained. They refused to let themselves become pawns on the Whig/Tory chessboard.

By 1706, Sophia was aged seventy-six so the likelihood of her ascending the throne decreased each year the considerably younger Anne managed to survive. Sophia's attitude towards becoming Queen was ambivalent. On the one hand she said that her dearest wish was to have inscribed on her tomb, 'Sophia, Queen of Great Britain'. On the other hand she had been on excellent terms with the exiled James II until his death, and she retained contact with his son, James Francis Edward, at St Germain (but then, so did most English politicians, hedging their bets in case the Stuart cause re-blossomed). It was through her Stuart blood that Sophia's claim to the throne lay – her brother Rupert had been Charles I's most famous cavalry commander in the Civil War. Some small part of her considered that the direct claim of James Francis Edward had its right to recognition.

George Lewis suffered from no such inhibitions. His share of Stuart blood had been overwhelmed by his father's Guelph characteristics. If England one day wanted him to become King, he would accept the offer – it would strengthen Hanover's position. If England changed her mind, it would not in the least upset him – Hanover would survive unaided. He was perfectly happy with his position as the undisputed ruler of an enlarged Hanover (Kalenberg had duly passed into his hands on the death of the Duke of Celle in 1705). He had his hunting and his mistresses to keep him even happier.

After 1706 and the passing of the Regency Bill, with the growing likelihood that George Lewis would be the next King, English politics became increasingly dominated by this consideration. So did the tactics of Marlborough as the commander-in-chief of the Grand Alliance. George Lewis was aware of his mounting importance on the general European stage and it

A portrait of the Duke of Marlborough attributed to Closterman. His brilliance as a strategist was responsible for the major successes of the Grand Alliance in the War of the Spanish Succession.

therefore came as an unpleasant surprise when, in 1708, Marlborough put considerations of his importance as the next probable King of England below those of the war effort as a whole.

George Lewis had been persuaded to take command of the armies of the Upper Rhine, which were in a bad state. He accepted the post with reluctance, fearing that the Rhine sector would be a side-show, that he would be left to re-organise its shattered armies while the glory and victory occurred in another area. This is precisely what happened. Without consulting George Lewis, Marlborough linked with his most forceful ally, Prince Eugène, and fought the successful battle of Oudenarde. It was some time before George Lewis forgave the great Duke for this deception. His chagrin was not lessened by the fact that his son George, with whom he was already on bad terms, played a prominent part in the battle, leading a gallant charge. Throughout 1708 and 1709, while others were covering themselves with glory, George Lewis struggled to re-organise the armies of the Upper Rhine. In so doing he revealed the energetic, disciplined side of his nature, normally so well camouflaged, which made him a good ruler of a despotic state such as Hanover.

By 1709, France was nearly on her knees, and peace negotiations started. But they soon broke down, basically because the Whigs who were still in power in England demanded too much of Louis XIV. In the meantime, France recovered some of her strength and the war continued. That negotiations collapsed due to English intransigence was an indication of how greatly England had already increased her power as a result of the war. Although the design of the Grand Alliance had been William III's, England had entered the war as one of the allies. But, by 1709, she was showing signs of becoming a leading European power. This can be attributed to Marlborough's genius, to the success of the British grenadiers as they row-towed-towed their way from Blenheim to Ramillies, from Oudenarde to Malplaquet (the bloodiest battle of all) and also to the surprising resilience shown by the English economy.

By 1710 – when George Lewis relinquished command of the Rhine armies in disgust – Marlborough's star was waning. During that year Queen Anne dismissed her leading Whig minister, Godolphin, whom she had never liked though he had served her nobly. In the ensuing election the Tories were returned to power with a large majority. A new battle started on the home front, to oust Marlborough from power, but it met with little response from the allies. However much they might have thwarted the great Duke in his past campaigns, they quailed at the prospect of removing from command the best general in Europe. George Lewis was among those who protested, showing that he could, on occasions, forgive those who had injured him. He wrote, 'I hope nothing will be capable of inducing the Queen to take the command of her armies from a general who has acquitted himself with so much glory and so much success, and in whose hands I shall always see it with pleasure.'

Marlborough's own assessment of George Lewis's position was more accurate – and sagacious. He wrote to his wife, the famous Sarah, 'You must not flatter yourself that the Elector of Hanover is capable of acting a vigorous part. I believe he will show that he esteems me; but at the same time, will be desirous of meddling as little as possible with the affairs of England, for which I cannot blame him, for not caring to have to do with so villainous a people.' Marlborough's bitterness, as revealed in the last sentence, is understandable. He was eventually removed from command, and there was every sign of a witch-hunt being mounted against him in England.

George Lewis continued to refrain from interfering in English affairs. However, in 1710, alarmed by the activities of the new Tory regime, he and his mother took one precaution. They despatched to London as their ambassador their most trusted and faithful minister, Baron Johann Caspar von Bothmar. He had instructions to keep his ear to the ground and to watch over Hanoverian interests.

The new Tory regime was led by Robert Harley, soon created Earl of Oxford and made Lord High Treasurer by Queen Anne. Oxford, a Whig turned Tory, was on the whole a moderate man, but he was secretive and he loved power and wine overmuch, attributes which tended to negate his moderation. His great rival was Henry St John, also soon ennobled as Viscount Bolingbroke, who held the office of Secretary of State, and who was anything but moderate. He was a scintillating orator, a sometimes profound political author and an arch-intriguer, while his womanising made George Lewis's affairs

'You must not flatter yourself that the Elector of Hanover is capable of acting a vigorous part'

Ramillies – after a long and
hard fight, Marlborough
gained a victory
comparable to that of
Blenheim, dispersing the
French and Bavarian
troops westwards.

54

assume the aspect of a country vicar's. In many ways Bolingbroke was a brilliant man and politician but he was flawed by his excesses; as a contemporary wrote, 'his faults are of the first magnitude'. Between him and Oxford there developed a bitter fight for power which was to have disastrous effects on the Tories.

It was Bolingbroke who entered into new negotiations with the French for a peace settlement. It was he who engineered the Treaty of Utrecht in 1713 which brought the War of the Spanish Succession to a conclusion. Retrospectively, it was a good treaty, a piece of statesmanship. It undoubtedly secured the British interests but, while it stripped France of her exorbitant power, it did not humiliate her. Thus no festering bitterness stayed with France and the European balance of power was not tipped too sharply in any direction.

At the time, the Treaty left an acrid taste in many mouths. The Whigs accused Bolingbroke of having thrown away all the advantages gained by Marlborough's victories. They said he had done this in a partisan and deliberate manner so that the peace would seem to be a Tory triumph, and because he wanted Louis XIV's help in securing a Stuart succession after Anne's death. The allies were just as vociferous in their denunciations. They accused Bolingbroke of entering into secret and separate negotiations with France, and, having done so, of proceeding to jettison their interests in favour of the British. Nobody was louder in his denunciations of the Treaty and its architect than George Lewis. However, in 1712, before the Treaty of Utrecht was ratified, the Tories had taken an action which they hoped would placate the House of Hanover. By an Act of Parliament, they had granted precedence over all British subjects to the Electress Sophia, the Elector George Lewis and his son the Electoral Prince George. Sophia and George Lewis accepted the honour but displayed no greater enthusiasm for the Tories than before.

As 1713 merged into 1714 and Queen Anne's health gave more cause for alarm, the question increasingly became – was there to be a Hanoverian Succession at all? It was not only Bolingbroke who played with the idea of a second Stuart restoration. It was widely known that Anne suffered from severe guilt feelings about her part in the deposing of her father,

James II. Indeed, she believed that her failure to have a living child after so many pregnancies was the judgment of heaven on her unfilial behaviour. But it was also widely known that Anne was staunch in her Protestant faith and her conviction that England must have a Protestant monarch. However, if James Francis Edward could be persuaded to become a Protestant, Anne would surely be only too delighted to make amends to her half-brother by repealing the Act of Settlement, while a Tory-dominated Parliament would also agree to the repeal.

Such were the Jacobite hopes early in 1714. Bolingbroke, as a result of the Treaty of Utrecht and George Lewis's disapproval, had become an ardent Jacobite. He hastened to France to consult James Francis Edward. His reception was not encouraging. The possible James III, dominated by a devout Catholic mother, had no intention of changing his religion. Nor, with typical Stuart inflexibility, had he any intention of bargaining with Parliament. Bolingbroke returned to England with his tail between his legs, for Anne would assuredly not agree to a Catholic successor, however strong her guilt feelings.

Then an event occurred which again raised Jacobite hopes. The Hanoverian supporters in England were worried by the blossoming of a pro-Stuart atmosphere. They decided that it would be an excellent idea to have at least one representative of the House of Hanover in England. Anne had shown that she was absolutely opposed to the presence of Sophia or George Lewis while she was alive, but what about the Electoral Prince George? He had earlier been created Duke of Cambridge (and given other titles), so he had the right to be summoned to Parliament as a Peer of the Realm. To be summoned, he would need to be in England. Then, if Anne should suddenly die, there would be at least one Hanoverian representative on the spot to take control of the situation.

The pro-Hanoverians managed to enlist Sophia's support for this plan. She wrote a letter which appeared to *demand* that her grandson be summoned to take his place in the House of Lords. It was the only tactical error made by Sophia in the long years of waiting for the English crown. When Anne heard the news she was furious. Although the writ of summons had technically to be issued, Anne wrote a long letter to Sophia making it plain that if the Electoral Prince George should follow it up, his

Robert Harley, Earl of Oxford, the self-indulgent Whig-turned-Tory whom Anne created Lord High Treasurer.

59

reception in England would be freezing. Not long after receiving this angry letter from Anne, on 8 June 1714, Sophia died, aged eighty-four. Thus she failed by less than two months to become Queen of Great Britain.

Despite the fact that George Lewis, now the heir-presumptive, had taken no hand in the affair of the summons, Queen Anne's fury and the way in which the business had been bungled brought the Hanoverian position to a new ebb. The affair also helped widen the bitter split among the Tories, for by no means all Tories were Jacobite adherents. And it hastened the downfall of the Earl of Oxford who had not supported Queen Anne in her rage. When Oxford went down, the man who would emerge on top would be Bolingbroke, and he favoured the Stuart Succession. In the event, Bolingbroke's triumph was short-lived. Anne finally dismissed Oxford on 27 July 1714, after an unseemly scene during which he and Bolingbroke hurled insults at each other over the head of the already desperately ill Queen. Bolingbroke enjoyed only two days of full power. These he failed to turn to his advantage, partly because he had alienated too many individuals and factions to be able to form a strong ruling clique. He was not helped in obtaining support for the Stuart claim by James Francis Edward's reiteration that he would never become a Protestant. Bolingbroke himself was uncertain which way to jump: he was a man of restless energy but in the crisis he did not show the necessary iron resolve or nerve to handle the situation.

Time was decidedly not on Bolingbroke's side. On 29 July, Anne's illness became worse and by 30 July, it was obvious that she was dying. The existing Cabinet, bereft of its titular leader Oxford, disunited under Bolingbroke, had no plan of action either for or against the Hanoverian Succession. It was left to three middle-of-the-road dukes to take action which they did most effectively. They weighed all the factors and came to the conclusion that the Hanoverian Succession had been ordained by Parliament; that the Stuart succession could lead to civil war; that this was to be avoided at all costs; therefore, the Hanoverians it must be. They obtained a majority Whig and Tory support for this view, including eventually that of Bolingbroke. They advised the dying Queen to appoint the Duke of Shrewsbury as her Lord High Treasurer, which she did. With

Henry St John, Viscount Bolingbroke, Oxford's rival in the fight for power, an unscrupulous intriguer who led a scandalous personal life.

Shrewsbury appointed, the Privy Councillors worked with lightning speed to ensure a peaceful Hanoverian succession. They strengthened the garrisons in such vital places as the Tower of London and Edinburgh Castle. They called out the militia in the City of London. They sealed all ports to prevent the arrival of Stuart arms or emissaries. They sent letters to Lord Mayors and Mayors, to army and navy commanders ordering them to be prepared for the death of the Queen and the succession of her lawful heir, the Elector of Hanover. For twelve hours, the messengers galloped in and out of Kensington Palace

where Anne lay dying. One of the most vital messengers carried news to the Elector's ambassador in London, Baron von Bothmar, keeping him abreast of events.

In the rest of the country, ordinary citizens debated the issue fiercely. Daniel Defoe described the ferment thus: 'If you chose to listen to your cookmaids and footmen in the kitchen, you shall hear them scolding and swearing and fighting among themselves, and when you think the noise is about beef and pudding, the dishwater or the kitchen staff, alas, you are mistaken; the feud is about who is for the Protestant Succession and who for the Pretender.' Undoubtedly, the Privy Councillors took the decision the majority of Englishmen wanted. Years of strife lay behind. Few wished them to re-appear. If there was little enthusiasm for the Hanoverians, there was less for the Stuart record of turmoil, or for a return of Catholicism, or for a monarch who had spent his life in enemy France. As Bolingbroke later wrote of the Stuart hopes, 'The fruit turned rotten the very moment it grew ripe.'

On 31 July, after their long labours, the Privy Councillors met again. Acquainted with the news that the Queen was sinking fast, they signed a letter which, with the approval of Baron von Bothmar, was sent post-haste to Hanover. It apprised the Elector of the fact that he would undoubtedly be King of England by the time he received it. It asked him 'to vouchsafe upon this first notice to favour this nation by your immediate presence'.

At six o'clock in the morning of 1 August 1714, further messengers were sent galloping from Kensington Palace to inform the Privy Councillors that the Queen had but a few hours to live. Before the Councillors could arrive from their homes in London – and it was a good gallop from rural Kensington to London proper – Anne had died. As the faithful Doctor Arbuthnot, who was with her to the end, wrote to Dean Swift, 'I believe sleep was never more welcome to a weary traveller than death was to her.'

3
Our Only Lawful and Rightful Liege Lord
1714-15

As QUEEN ANNE'S ATTENDANTS mourned her death in Kensington Palace, they heard the sound of cannon thundering in the distance. The guns were not announcing an armed uprising, they were being fired in the City of London to proclaim the accession of George I. The proclamation was read soon after midday to the vast crowd that had gathered outside St James's Palace. The kettledrums rolled and the trumpets sounded, then the herald declaimed, '... with one full voice and consent of tongue and heart ... the High and Mighty Prince George Elector of Brunswick-Luneberg is now by the death of our late sovereign of Happy Memory, become our only lawful and rightful liege Lord, George, by the Grace of God King of Great Britain, France and Ireland ... God save the King'. (The title 'King of France' was a remnant of past centuries, retained more in a spirit of absent-mindedness than of present or future reality.) Later, on 1 August, the proclamation was read in the major English towns and cities. On 5 August, George was proclaimed King in Edinburgh, and the following day in Dublin. The Privy Councillors had performed their task well, and the news was received, if not with enormous enthusiasm, at least with equanimity.

Even before the proclamation was read, the Privy Councillors continued to perform their task of ensuring the peaceful Hanoverian Succession. The Regency Act of 1706 had provided the instruments for an efficient hand-over. As the proclamation itself was being prepared in one room of St James's Palace, in another the Privy Councillors were solemnly opening the three sealed documents containing the list of Regents. This list, as decreed in the Regency Act, had previously been compiled by George Lewis. The documents were opened in the presence of Baron von Bothmar and another Hanoverian representative. They were found to contain mainly the names of moderate Whigs who had long supported the Hanoverian Succession and a few moderate Tories who had done likewise. Among the omissions were several Whigs who had previously held high office, the name of Bolingbroke and also that of the Duke of Marlborough. The omission of the leading Whigs proved that George had a mind of his own and was not prepared to be a Whig tool. The omission of Bolingbroke was not surprising but it spelled his immediate doom, even if he had eventually

66

signed the document ordering the Hanoverian Succession. The omission of the great Duke of Marlborough was more surprising. It was regarded as an indication that George had not altogether forgiven his actions during the 1708 campaigns.

However, Marlborough was soon in favour again, though his days of enormous power were ended. He and Sarah were in exile in 1714 but they set out for England on hearing the news that the Queen was dangerously ill. They landed in Dover on the day of her death and were given a triumphal 'Welcome home' by the people of the town, and a few days later by the citizens of London. Following this gratifying evidence of their popular support, on 6 August, George indicated that all was finally forgiven. On that day, from Hanover of course, he signed a document re-instating Marlborough as the Captain-General of the British forces. It was the first document he signed as King of England. It was appropriate because Marlborough had (on the whole, in his later years) been loyal to the Hanoverian Succession. Certainly no man was more responsible than he for the present peaceful, secure state of England and Hanover.

From within hours of Anne's death, the country had a Regency fully empowered to rule. The hand-over of power had occurred more smoothly than even the most optimistic Hanoverian supporter could have dared to hope. But for the rest of August and half of September, the country remained without its actual monarch. The letter written to George as Anne lay dying had requested him to favour the country with his immediate presence, but he showed no inclination to hasten towards his new kingdom. Why should he? He was fifty-four years old and his life had been spent in Hanover. Moreover, as has been so felicitously written, 'not a mouse had stirred against him in England, in Ireland or in Scotland'. In France, a financially-straitened Louis XIV was showing no signs of backing James Francis Edward with material aid, even if he had officially recognised him as the rightful King of England on Anne's death. Besides, George had his own affairs to put in order. It is significant that in the months leading up to Anne's death, when England was consumed by the question of who should succeed her, George's own attention was focussed on the annexation of the two small states of Bremen and Verden. For him, Hanover always came first, England was of secondary importance.

'Not a mouse had stirred against him in England, in Ireland or in Scotland'

Very slowly, George organised his affairs in Hanover. He issued an Ordinance delegating authority to the Hanoverian Privy Councillors including his brother, Ernest Augustus. But final authority rested with him, and all important decisions were to be referred to him in London. It is a measure of how securely despotic a state Hanover was that nobody challenged his authority during the years he was in England. Finally, by 31 August, George could find no reason to remain longer in Hanover and he set forth for his new kingdom. His progress was still very leisurely and it was not until 18 September that he landed at Greenwich.

His arrival was delayed by thick fog, and it was in swirling mist that, in the early evening of 18 September, he set foot on English soil as its lawful king. Apart from the welcoming dignitaries and peers of the realm, he was greeted by a large and reasonably enthusiastic crowd. A mass of candles and torch-

A view of Greenwich, where George finally arrived to take up the crown, to be greeted by a typical London fog, as well as the dignitaries awaiting his arrival.

68

lights brightened the scene, fitfully illuminating the splendid new additions to Greenwich Palace recently constructed by Sir Christopher Wren. The monarch was subjected to a lengthy poem of which we will give only a brief extract:

> Hail mighty George! auspicious smiles they Reign,
> Thee long we wish'd. Thee at last we gain.

The standard of poetry was such that George might have been able to grasp it, though his appreciation of the verbal and visual arts was later crystallised in the immortal remark made in his execrable English, 'I hate all boets and bainters.' Even greater than his hatred of poetry and painting was his dislike of pomp and ceremony. But from Greenwich, George proceeded to London, where he had to endure a state entry into the City. He was accompanied by his son George (soon created Prince of Wales), surrounded by the Life Guards-in-Waiting and two thousand members of the nobility and gentry. According to Lady Mary Wortley Montagu, he arrived in London also surrounded 'by all his German ministers and playfellows male and female'.

In fact George was not surrounded by *all* his female play-fellows. His *maîtresse en titre*, Mademoiselle Schulenberg, refused to accompany him, as Lady Mary also noted, 'fearing that the people of England, who, she thought, were accustomed to use their kings barbarously, might chop off his head in the first fortnight'. However, Madame Kielmansegge showed more spirit, or less stupidity, and was present to comfort George during his first days in his new country. George was later reported as saying of these first days, presumably in German as his English never reached such a neat standard, 'This is a very odd country. The first morning after my arrival at St James's I looked out of the window, and saw a park with walls, and a canal, and were told they were mine. The next day, the ranger of *my* park, sent me a brace of fine carp out of *my* canal, and I was told I must give five guineas to the man, for bringing me *my own* carp out of *my own* canal in *my own* park.'

Included among 'the playfellows' were the two Turkish servants, Mustapha and Mahomet. They were described as procurers rather than servants by some sections of the English Court, while all were astonished that George should be so

The Grand Staircase at
Kensington Palace: on the
landing are George's
beloved Turkish servants
Mahomet and Mustapha
(right) and his elegant
page Ulric, in Polish
dress (far left).

friendly with the Turks, whatever their true function. It was
probably in part due to his shyness that George forged so firm a
bond with them. They had proved themselves loyal, were
mentally undemanding, and the terms of the relationship were
clearly defined between master and foreign subordinates. Also
among the entourage that arrived in London were eighteen
cooks, but only one washerwoman, which casts an interesting
light on Hanoverian eating habits and standards of cleanliness.

The most important people in the party were George's
German ministers. Of these, the man who wielded the greatest
influence was his Prime Minister, Baron von Bernstorff. He had
served George faithfully for years – it was Bernstorff who had
drawn up the terms of the divorce from Sophia Dorothea and
stage-managed the whole affair. Of the other men who wielded
great power in the early years of George's reign, one was
already in England, Baron von Bothmar. His power was
ready-made because he had served the Hanoverian interest in
London so well, and in the process had acquired a vital knowledge of English politicians. Bothmar knew who was to be
trusted and who was not, and his recommendations were
mainly accepted by George.

The other key figure travelled from Hanover, though his
knowledge of English politics was equal to Bothmar's. He was
a man called Jean de Robethon, a French Huguenot refugee
who had been confidential secretary to William III and later
found his way to Hanover, where he had been Bernstorff's
private secretary. It was as George's private secretary that he
officially came to England. The term 'private' or 'confidential'
secretary covered a wide field of activity. Robethon was in fact
an arch-intriguer, the eighteenth-century backstairs politician
who had his ear to every keyhole, his eye on every letter, who
moved secretly and silently, manipulating events. Robethon's
loyalty, once given, remained secure, and he had worked tirelessly to ensure George's accession to the English throne. He
was to work as tirelessly for George (and himself) in England.
George rewarded the devotion, leaning as heavily on Robethon's advice as on Bothmar's. It was not long before Robethon
was the most hated man on the English political scene. He was
described as 'a prying, impertinent, venemous creature, for ever
crawling in some slimy intrigue'.

70

With George in England, the Regency had fulfilled its function. A few days after his arrival, George produced his list of ministers, drawn up mainly on the advice of Bothmar and Robethon. George himself had, in his list of Regents, already strongly indicated that his favour lay towards the Whigs who had supported the Hanoverian Succession. The vital ministerial list extended this unsurprising preference. The Tories were out, only one of the new ministers being of their party. And George, showing he had a mind of his own when he chose to exercise it, had vetoed Bothmar's suggestion that he might have a mixed ministry, retaining some of the pro-Hanoverian Tories.

The field of Whigs was widened, and there was one surprising inclusion among the new ministers – James, Earl Stanhope. He was a complicated character, part bluff, hearty soldier, part sophisticated European. He was appointed Secretary of State for the Southern Department. (There were then two Secretaries of State, for the Northern and Southern Departments, and the former was the more important.) One historic office, that of Lord High Treasurer, was allowed to lapse. Ostensibly this was to prevent any single person gaining power as had Oxford and Bolingbroke, but it did not in practice work out that way. James, Earl Stanhope, proved to be a formidable politician, in the field of foreign affairs one of England's great Foreign Secretaries. His inclusion in George's first ministerial list can probably be attributed to Jean de Robethon, whom he knew well.

Another man who swam to the top in his first temporary ministry was Charles, Viscount Townshend, who was appointed Secretary of State for the Northern Department. Again, Townshend's rise was due to Hanoverian influence, in this instance to Baron von Bothmar. Townshend was a second generation nobleman, very conscious of his birth and breeding. He had a strong, forceful character, capable of noble rudeness when the occasion demanded and sometimes when it did not. He was not addicted to the contemporary vices of excessive wining and womanising and was scrupulously honest. When he was finally forced out of office, it was agreed that he departed not one penny richer than the day he had first assumed power – a rare achievement in the eighteenth century. Townshend's family home was in Norfolk and his brother-in-law was a

James, Earl Stanhope, painted by Kneller. An outstanding politician, his meteoric career in foreign affairs began with his appointment by George to the office of Secretary of State for the Southern Department.

73

Charles, Viscount
Townshend, Secretary of
State for the Northern
Department, notable for
his strength of character
and rare honesty. Like
Stanhope, he owed his
position to Hanoverian
influence.

gentleman called Robert Walpole who obtained a post in the new ministry, too. Townshend was to be remembered by future generations as 'Turnip Townshend', the man who publicised the value of turnips as a winter feed for sheep and cattle, and thereby helped revolutionise English farming. (Previously the animals had been slaughtered in the autumn for lack of winter food.) But in 1714 and the years following, he was not known by his mocking nickname, and was anything but vegetable in action.

It is interesting to note that George's list of ministers was accepted without question or demur. Yet the excluded Tories had a majority in the House of Commons. They were the party voted into power by the electorate, however limited that might be. But nobody raised constitutional doubts or queried George's right to appoint the ministers he wanted, which demonstrates how great the King's personal power remained, despite the limitations imposed by the Act of Settlement. It was obvious that an election must be held soon, but in the meantime the King's appointed ministry held sway.

The coronation took place at Westminster Abbey on 20 October 1714. It was a further occasion to make George flinch. But the English loved pomp and ceremony, and George had to endure the full splendour of the coronation, 'in his royal robes of crimson velvet, furr'd with ermine and bordered with rich broad, gold lace, wearing the collar of the order of St George ... and on his head a cap of estate turn'd up with ermine, adorned with a circle of gold, enrich'd with diamonds ... under a canopy borne by the Barons of the Cinque Ports, his train borne by four noblemen's eldest sons'. When the traditional moment came for the Archbishop of Canterbury to demand the consent of the people to George's crowning, Lady Dorchester (ex-mistress of James II) turned to Lady Cowper (who recorded the incident in her diary) and said, 'Does the old Fool think that anybody will say no to his question, when there are so many drawn swords?' Also during the long proceedings, Lady Dorchester noted the Duchess of Portsmouth (a surviving mistress of Charles II) and Lady Orkney (mistress to William III) among the congregation, whereupon she made the splendid remark, 'Good God! Who would have thought we three whores would have met together here.'

74

Charles
2 Vis.^t Townshend

There was one sector of the community that did not require drawn swords to convince them that George's was the rightfully crowned head. They were the Dissenters. The term covered any person who refused to accept the Act of Uniformity of 1662 which had in effect stated that people must conform to the rites of the Church of England or suffer the consequences. By the Toleration Act of 1689, non-Anglican Protestants such as Quakers and Baptists had been granted certain religious liberty, and the term Dissenter had come to mean only Protestant nonconformists, not Catholics or Jews. But in the last months of Queen Anne's reign, Bolingbroke had introduced the Schism Bill to deny Dissenters the right to educate their children as they wished, in their own schools. It was then a retrograde, divisive Bill, drawing on the strength of religious hatred and intolerance and it would have destroyed the Dissenters as a community. Bolingbroke himself was not an intolerant man. He introduced the Bill as a political manœuvre, one of his aims being the destruction of his hated rival Oxford who came from a Dissenting background. In the process he helped wreck the Tories who were rent even further asunder by the internal struggles engendered. Literally, as Anne died, the Schism Bill was due to become law. While her death did not remove it from the statute book, the terms became a dead letter. Consequently, George had the ardent support of the Dissenters throughout his reign.

Apart from the Dissenters as a group, there was one man who whole-heartedly welcomed the accession of George Lewis. That man's motives were neither political nor religious. They were personal and musical, because he was George Frederick Handel. He was of course German, though not Hanoverian, by birth, and in his early twenties had been appointed *Kappelmeister* to the Court at Herrenhausen. But in 1711, at the age of twenty-six, he had come to England, where his opera *Rinaldo* was first performed and received with rapture. Handel liked London, whereas he had not greatly cared for the Hanoverian Court – he shared the imprisoned Sophia Dorothea's views about its dullness and lack of artistic feeling. Consequently, he prolonged his visit to London. The more he prolonged his sojourn in the English capital, the less the idea of returning to Hanover appealed to him. The longer the *Kappelmeister*,

George I in his coronation robes, shown in a painting after Kneller. His crown, orb and sceptre are seen on the table at his side.

77

Music in George I's Reign

Music was one of George's interests and his visits to the opera were among his few public appearances. Handel, his *Kappelmeister* in Hanover, seduced by his London successes, spent more and more time in the English capital. On George's accession, both parties benefited: Handel remained in London and was rewarded by an increase in the pension originally granted to him by Queen Anne.

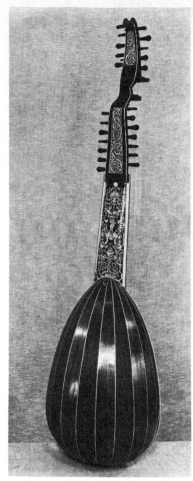

ABOVE RIGHT A theorboe, a member of the lute family.
ABOVE LEFT Handel rehearses an oratorio.
RIGHT A German spinet, built inside an ebony writing-box decorated with silver.

LEFT Thomas Hudson's portrait of Handel, now in Windsor Castle.
BELOW A painting by Philip Mercier of a contemporary music party.

crowned with further artistic glory as the result of his English triumphs, stayed away from Hanover, the less pleased grew the Elector. (And if George Lewis hated all poets and painters, he showed some interest in music and opera.) The situation was reaching a crisis point, at least for Handel, who saw the dullness of Herrenhausen re-enveloping him, when George Lewis became the rightful George I of England. With his master ensconced in London, Handel was able to remain, to his own personal satisfaction and the great benefit of English music.

The loyalty of other sectors of the community, including some who had attended the coronation, remained in doubt. On coronation day, there were rumblings from Stuart supporters, with rioting in Bristol, Chippenham, Norwich, Reading and Birmingham marking disapproval of the Hanoverian Succession. There was a fair number of people in all parts of the country and all walks of life who endorsed the sentiment expressed in the contemporary doggerel:

> God in his wrath sent Saul to punish Jewry;
> And George to England in greater fury.

As 1715 dawned, the Stuart support remained disorganised and without a great leader convinced of its just and lawful rightness. There were those convinced of the inviolability of the Stuart claims, but they lacked powers of real leadership. Those who could have provided the leadership, such as Bolingbroke, were still not certain whom to support. In the meantime, those who had the power, the Whigs in the King's confidence, continued to exercise it. With each month George I stayed unchallenged on the throne, the Stuart hopes of deposing him lessened.

At the beginning of 1715, Parliament was dissolved and an election called. The King issued a highly partisan proclamation, calling upon the electorate to return to Westminster only those who had showed 'a firmness to the Protestant Succession, when it was in danger'. The limited electorate duly responded to the royal call by returning a large majority, about one hundred and fifty, for the Whigs. The revulsion from the Tories was occasioned as much by their recent record of internal dissension, by the hope that George and the Whigs would bring stability, as by love or enthusiasm for them. But the election results were

The House of Commons in session in 1710, painted by Pieter Tillemans.

another nail in the coffin of Stuart hopes. Their hopes had not been assisted by a counter-proclamation issued by James Francis Edward. In this he had reiterated that he would never become a Protestant, and had failed to guarantee the right to Protestant worship for the majority of his prospective subjects. On the delicate, crucial subject of religion, even his most ardent supporters – while respecting the Pretender's own faith and believing that he would show toleration towards the Protestants – wished fervently that he would keep his mouth shut until he had obtained the throne.

The new Whig Parliament met in March 1715. One of its first actions was to impeach four leading Tory ministers from the last regime, including the Earl of Oxford, Viscount Boling-broke and the Duke of Ormonde. The action was not necessary as the King had patently shown that he had no confidence in them. But it kept the Whig supporters happy. The Tory villains responsible for the ignoble Treaty of Utrecht and favouring the unwanted Stuart succession would receive their just desserts. More importantly, it kept four possible Stuart leaders away from the centre of the fray at the moment of crisis. In fact, Oxford completely denied that he had committed any treasonable actions, or that he had favoured the Stuarts. Nonetheless, he was imprisoned in the Tower of London, though he was not badly treated and was eventually acquitted and released in 1717. But Bolingbroke and Ormonde saved the Whigs the trouble of lengthy impeachment proceedings by fleeing to France.

Bolingbroke went at the end of March, before the Whigs had moved against him. With hindsight, it is easy to say that Boling-broke should have stayed put like his enemy Oxford, and similarly denied his guilt. Undoubtedly he would have been imprisoned, but his prospects of eventually wielding power again would have been improved. At the time, it was not obvious that the Stuart cause was doomed and that the Hano-verians had come to stay. One attribute Bolingbroke possessed in high measure was a feeling for the mood of the country. He was right in believing that after only a few months of Hanover-ian rule, discontent was rife on many fronts. At the higher levels, the Tories, already rejected by George himself, were being systematically removed from offices both major and minor by the Whigs. This obviously produced a reservoir of bitter anti-Hanoverian sentiment, because the Whigs were now synonymous with the Hanoverians. At the lower levels, George's own popularity, which had never been high, was fast diminishing. His cold, reserved nature, his lack of charm, his dislike of ceremony, had done nothing to endear him to the populace, while at all levels the rumours about the band of Hanoverians surrounding the King, with their 'cacophonous, outlandish German names', their corruption and their rapacity were widespread. It seemed that England was in danger of being taken over by a pack of grasping, unattractive foreigners.

'Their cacophonous, outlandish German names'

Apart from recognising the re-blossoming pro-Stuart sentiment, Bolingbroke had personal reasons for deciding to support the Pretender. He could see no immediate chance of regaining power under a Hanoverian king, whereas he could see every prospect of sweeping back to the summit if he utilised the discontent and secured the throne for James Francis Edward. Then there was the deep-rooted feeling that the Pretender's claim was more legitimate than George of Hanover's. There was also the possibility that he might prove the better king.

In the event, Bolingbroke opted for the Pretender, although characteristically he hesitated several days after arriving in France before finally committing himself. Unfortunately, when he did commit himself, the Pretender failed to utilise the services of the ablest man and politician in his service. James Francis Edward was surrounded by the second-rate and sycophantic minds that were drawn to a Court in exile. He was dominated by his devout, not to say bigoted Catholic mother, Mary of Modena; hence the repeated statements about his never becoming a Protestant and the failure to guarantee Protestant worship in England. He neither gave personal access nor paid attention at a distance to the man who might have transformed his Court and cause into a first-class enterprise.

James Francis Edward preferred the advice of such men as the Duke of Ormonde. The latter had been born in Dublin in 1665, had supported William III against James II but had become more and more Tory and pro-Stuart as the years went by. Had he possessed any qualities of leadership he could have led the counter-*coup* when Anne died, because he had a great name and was then Captain-General of the forces, having succeeded the

83

deposed Marlborough. But, as a contemporary wrote, 'such designs need a hero, and that was what the Duke of Ormonde was not'. Personally he was brave, personally he now believed in the Stuarts, but he was weak and timorous in coming to a decision. If somebody suggested something he would consider it, if somebody suggested something else he would consider that, and in the meantime the vital moment had passed. But Ormonde was more to the liking of the Pretender than the brilliant, erratic, politically sagacious Bolingbroke.

Bolingbroke *was* politically sagacious. What he can be accused of in joining the Pretender's service is underestimating the strength and will of the Whigs in power in England. He was not really to know until he got to France that James Francis Edward was such a typical Stuart, weak but obstinate, brave but incompetent. He was certainly not to know that his own valuable advice would be so totally ignored. But Bolingbroke might have shown more appreciation of the fact that there was a decisive ministry in London under the firm control of Townshend and Stanhope, convinced that George must remain king, and that this ministry had an excellent, equally convinced ambassador in Paris – Lord Stair, of Glencoe Massacre notoriety – whose spies kept him informed on Jacobite moves. (This was not a difficult task as the Jacobites were notoriously indiscreet.) And he should have realised that the increasingly important mercantile class was pro-Hanoverian; indeed, all business sectors supported George, believing he could provide the necessary stability to allow the English economy to continue on its booming upward path. Bolingbroke surely should have been aware of the religious aspect which troubled many people, even those whose emotions tended towards the supposedly more glamorous and legitimate Stuarts. It was he who observed, 'England would as soon have a Turk as a Roman Catholic for King.' Despite all the evidence to the contrary, Bolingbroke hoped that the Pretender could be persuaded to change his religion and become a Protestant.

The Pretender himself realised that his moment had arrived but, as Bolingbroke wrote, 'he dwelt in a maze of unrealities, out of which he was never strong or bold enough to break' and 'he was a man who expected every moment to set sail for England or Scotland, but who did not very well know for

Kneller's official portrait of George I in his robes of state, showing the east end of Westminster Abbey in the background.

which'. Bolingbroke rightly urged James Francis Edward to concentrate on the former country, saying that success lay in gaining 'the purse and strength of England'. He also urged him to issue a proclamation appealing directly to the populace, seeking their support for the re-accession of the rightful Stuart Kings of England. But the idea of appealing to the inferior masses was not one which attracted the Pretender. Its sound good sense was not comprehended by a Stuart imbued with a belief in the divine right of kings. To a degree, the Pretender's hand was forced by the Scots, or at least by the Highland nobles, who precipitously raised the flag of rebellion. The Highland response was not surprising. In the first place, there was the emotional historic blood tie of the Stuarts as Scotland's own monarchs. Then, many of the Highland nobles were Catholics, and most of them were disenchanted with the Act of Union.

This historic Act, which, as Daniel Defoe said, was 'the nicest and greatest concern' of the age, had been passed in 1707. In the years preceding the ratification it had become increasingly obvious that the idea of a dual monarchy – one king or queen as head of state of England and Scotland, but the two countries otherwise remaining separate – could not continue. Either the countries must separate entirely – and probably return to their former warring status – or there must be a greater degree of union. After years of politicking, argument and negotiation, with the Scots on the one hand shouting against 'England, insolent and proud like hell, Whose saucie boldness nought but blows can quell' and the English describing their northern neighbours as 'proud, arrogant, vainglorious, boasters, bloody barbarous and inhuman butchers' – an agreement was finally reached in 1707.

By the terms of the Act of Union, the Scots gave up their own Parliament, in which, prior to the negotiations, they had taken little interest. They agreed to send representatives to the single Parliament at Westminster, though they retained their own Church, judiciary and laws. In return for this merger, the commercial restrictions on Scotland as a 'foreign country' were lifted, and henceforward she shared freely in the English and colonial markets. English financial assistance was also guaranteed to pay off the Scottish national debt and the debts accrued in the disastrous Darien scheme. In the long-term, Scotland, as

'England, insolent and proud like hell, Whose saucie boldness nought but blows can quell'

a poor, under-developed country, benefited from the Act of Union (though not all Scots would agree with this generally accepted verdict). Short-term, because Scotland was a poor country and had not therefore the resources to take advantage of the benefits, the results were neither obvious nor encouraging. Many Scots, and not only Highlanders, felt that they had gained nothing from the Act of Union and had lost a great deal – their independence.

It was, of course, as a result of the Act of Union that the title 'Great Britain' came into being and the overall term 'British'. It was thus that the Electress Sophia, writing after 1707, was able to express her desire to have 'Sophia, Queen of Great Britain', rather than 'England', inscribed on her tomb. But by 1715, many Scots had no wish to be British. They felt that their only hope for the future lay with a Stuart re-accession which would, they believed, bring with it a renewed degree of autonomy, if not a return to full independence.

4
Wicked and Traitorous Measures
1715-16

IT WAS AT BRAEMAR – where the earls of Mar traditionally held a great summer hunt – that on 6 September 1715, the standard of rebellion was raised by the current Earl of Mar. Earlier, during the hunting festivities, Mar had waxed eloquent on 'that cursed Act of Union' (which he had regrettably had a hand in shaping), whereby Scotland had been 'delivered into the hands of the English'. He had been similarly eloquent on the necessity of establishing 'upon the thrones of these Realms the Chevalier St George' who had 'the undoubted right to the Crown, had promised to hear their Grievances and would redress their wrongs'. With final eloquence, if not accuracy, he had spoken of the simultaneous rising which would occur in England, and of the powerful assistance, both financial and military, which would arrive from France.

The raising of the standard was witnessed by a crowd of six thousand or a group of sixty – the numbers varied wildly according to the political sympathy of the writer. It was also accompanied by what was regarded as an evil omen. As the flag was raised, the gilt ball on the top of the pole fell to the ground. Nonetheless, Mar had proclaimed for the Pretender, the future James III of Great Britain, and he had gained the promise of support from a number of pro-Jacobite nobles and chieftains. Included among them were some of the great names of Scotland – the Marquesses of Huntly and Tullibardine, the Earls of Errol, Linlithgow and Seaforth, Lords Drummond and Ogilvy, Gordon of Auchintoul and Campbell of Glendaruel.

Having unfurled the flag, Mar set about rallying his tenants to the cause, instead of the other way round. The tenants did not respond over-willingly to the battle cry of the man whose nick-name was 'Bobbing Jack' (because of his endlessly shifting allegiance). Mar obtained some support, from his own tenantry and from the nobles who had promised their allegiance. In the early stages of the rebellion he acted with promptness – for a man of such indecisive character. On 14 September, the vital city of Perth fell to his forces. Had Mar then marched on Edinburgh, it would have undoubtedly fallen to him, and he would have had the moral advantage of the capital city under his control. He would also have had the material advantage of the badly-needed arms and ammunition which were stored in Edinburgh Castle. There was a plot to capture the Castle from

PREVIOUS PAGES James Francis Edward Stuart, the Old Pretender, lands at Peterhead; an engraving by Peter Schenk.

LEFT John, Earl of Mar, leading figure in the movement to restore the Stuarts. He bitterly resented the Act of Union of 1707.

within the city, before Mar could arrive, but it was a botched affair like most of the Jacobite plans, and even the ill-prepared and unalert garrison had no difficulty in suppressing it. Mar himself had exhausted his capacity for prompt action by taking Perth. For several weeks he dillied and dallied there, issuing edicts and proclamations of which nobody took any notice, because he had neither the will nor the means to enforce them.

The real hope for the Jacobite success lay with France – the French money and arms so lavishly promised by Mar before the rebellion started. But five days before he raised the standard, these hopes had been dealt a mortal blow. On 1 September, Louis XIV had died. As Bolingbroke said of his hopes for the Stuart cause, they 'sank as he declined and died as he expired'. The new Regent of France was known to favour a reconciliation with the Hanoverians, believing it would help his country more than a renewed war with England. Despite the fact that it was certain that France would not act immediately on behalf of the Jacobites, if Mar had proceeded with decision and resolution, the situation could have been radically changed. If he had gained control of all Scotland and the still strongly Catholic North of England, the French Regent might have been persuaded to send some support, and waverers in other parts of England might have descended on the Jacobite side of the fence.

One of his ministers wrote to George I, 'If any disgrace befall your Majesty's troops in Scotland, insurrection will immediately follow in England in many places, and probably the Pretender will be encouraged to land here, too. On the other hand, if the rebels get no advantage in Scotland, my conjecture is, there will be no considerable rising in England.' It was a fair assessment of the situation. There was no wild enthusiasm for the Pretender in England, but there was equally little for the Hanoverians. There were large numbers of people who were uncommitted, waiting on events. However, if Mar had shown signs of real success, the pro-Hanoverian forces in England would undoubtedly have rallied more strongly than they did. And the majority of the English population would have followed them for the same reasons they had accepted the Hanoverian Succession in the first place – the fear of a prolonged civil war, the desire for stability, the hatred of France, of Catholicism and of the dreaded papal authority. Nonetheless,

The Old Pretender, in a later portrait by Trevisani. He is shown with his son, who became famous as 'Bonnie Prince Charlie'.

greater decision on Mar's part could have made the success or failure of the rebellion a much closer run thing than it was.

In the circumstances as they were, no great panic occurred in England, and the stock market – that barometer of confidence – remained buoyant. However, there was justified concern, and several known or suspected Jacobite nobles and gentry were promptly arrested by the King's ministers to prevent their raising the standard in England. There was particular concern about the strength of the army, or more accurately about the weakness of England's military forces. But Stanhope was at one with Bolingbroke on the subject of where the Pretender should attack. Like Bolingbroke, he knew that England was the key to success, and he retained the bulk of the small army at home. He sent reinforcements to the West Country – a notoriously pro-Jacobite area – which were easily able to repulse the attempted landings by the Duke of Ormonde in Devonshire in October and December of 1715. Thus ended the disorganised Jacobite plans for simultaneous risings in England and Scotland. They were quashed in England as much by the lack of response from the West countrymen as by Stanhope's firm action. Notedly Jacobite the West might be, always prepared to drink to 'The King over the water'; but in the event few men were prepared to risk their lives for so uncertain a cause.

By October, Mar held most of Scotland for the Pretender. The country cannot be precisely said to have been under his control, as he was incapable of controlling anything or anybody efficiently. And it would have taken a man of political and military genius truly to have controlled the Scottish lords and clans, with their endless history of internecine warfare and individual greed. But the Highlands had come out for the Pretender, apart from Argyle's territories in the west and Sutherland's in the north. Much of the Lowlands had similarly proclaimed for James III, notably the Border lairds and nobles. The cities and areas that stayed loyal to the Hanoverians were round Edinburgh, Glasgow and Stirling. Glasgow had not then assumed the importance it was to attain with the coming of industrialisation, but it was one of under-populated Scotland's larger towns. Edinburgh, of course, remained vital as the capital city, while Stirling was crucial because of its geographical position as the gateway to both Highlands and Lowlands.

Battle of Dumblain.

The March of the Kings Forces and Cannon to Perth.

In October, Mar had approximately seven thousand men nominally under his command – some estimates put the figure at sixteen thousand but this seems improbably high. Undeniably, he had a large numerical superiority over the Duke of Argyle who had affirmed his loyalty to King George and had been put in command of the royal forces in Scotland. These royalist forces consisted of about fourteen hundred men with whom Argyle had to hold Stirling, defend Edinburgh and meet any thrust the Jacobites might make. Argyle himself was gloomy about the prospects, and he wrote to Townshend in London, 'I must end with insisting on considerable reinforcements, for without it, or a miracle, not only this country will be utterly destroyed but the rest of his Majesty's dominions put in extremest danger.' As events matured, Argyle needed neither large reinforcements nor a miracle. Mar's incompetence, the Jacobite lack of money and arms, the inevitable quarrels that erupted between the noble Scottish lords, came to his rescue.

Having done nothing in particular for the whole of October, Mar finally decided that a detachment of his forces should be sent south to join up with the Lowlanders. On 1 November, this combined Highland-Lowland force – disobeying Mar's instructions, which had been to wheel back up to Stirling – decided to cross the border into England. The decision was reached only after bitter wrangling among its leaders, and the primary impulse was the old freebooting Border instinct – 'Why the devil not into England, where there is both meat, men and money?' There proved to be little meat, men or money for the Jacobites in England. However, a section of the invaders joined up with the small army of the pro-Jacobite Northumbrian lords who had raised the standard for the Pretender. This joint Anglo-Scottish force had no clear plan of campaign. The idea was that they should strike for Liverpool, as a port and a good rallying-point for the Welsh Jacobites. Accordingly, they marched across Northumberland, into Cumberland, down through Westmorland into Lancashire. They met no resistance but they gained the minimum amount of support from the local inhabitants, including the Catholics.

At Preston, the Anglo-Scottish force was halted by a Hanoverian force under General Wills, which had been sent into the area by Stanhope. There was some brief and in one

General Cathcart, who acted as second-in-command to the Duke of Argyle, shown in this portrait by John Wootton with the field of Sherriffmuir in the background.

97

quarter bitter, fighting, but the Anglo-Scottish force was appallingly led and General Wills had little difficulty in defeating it. On 13 November, the remaining Jacobites – some had already disappeared home across the border – surrendered to General Wills. They numbered 75 English and 143 Scottish lords and about 1,400 troops, a thousand of whom were Scots. Thus, at Preston ended the invasion of England and the Jacobite hopes in that country.

On the same day, the battle of Sheriffmuir was fought in Scotland. Having received the news of the failure of the Duke of Ormonde's first landing in Devonshire, Mar had decided he must do something north of the border. On the fatal day of 13 November, his troops met the Duke of Argyle's at Sheriffmuir, which lies outside the town of Dunblane, five miles to the north of Stirling. The weather was bitterly cold, which was to the advantage of the Scots who were more accustomed to the conditions than the hastily assembled, mainly English troops. Mar retained his numerical superiority, having by this time some twelve thousand men, while Argyle's force was only three thousand. Neither leader showed outstanding military genius. It was said of Argyle, who had trained under the great Marlborough, that he was a better Christian than he was a general. Without doubt, Mar should have gained a decisive victory which could have tipped the scales towards the Jacobites. But nobody won the day. After some bitter fighting in the freezing weather, both sides left the field of Sheriffmuir. The result of the battle was wryly expressed in a Jacobite song:

> There's some say that we wan,
> Some say that they wan,
> And some say that nane wan ata, man;
> There's but ae thing, I'm sure,
> That, at Shirramuir,
> A battle there was, that I saw, man,
> And we ran, and they ran,
> And they ran, and we ran,
> And we ran, and they ran awa, man.

By failing to gain a decisive victory, by running away, the Jacobite hopes in Scotland were also doomed. Mar himself noted – as others before and after him – that the Highlanders,

98

THE
Battle
of
PRESTON

however brave they might be in battle, had one unfortunate tendency, and that was 'generally after an action they return home'. If the action showed no signs of leading anywhere, they certainly returned home.

At the battle of Sheriffmuir, 'the heart of the rebellion was broke', as a contemporary historian accurately observed, but the star of the show had yet to arrive. James Francis Edward, the Pretender, was then aged twenty-seven, 'tall and lean, a prominent chin, wide mouth, big nose, narrow oval face'. He had left his French Court at the end of October *en route* for his true kingdom, but it was not until 22 December 1715, that he finally landed at Peterhead in Aberdeenshire. Evading Lord Stair's efficient network of spies in France and atrocious weather had delayed his sailing until late December. When he finally set foot in Scotland, he was less than enchanted with what he found – as was his relation George of Hanover on arrival in England. The Scots, like the English with George, were unenthusiastic about him. An anonymous pamphleteer described reactions thus:

> When we saw the man whom they called our king, we found ourselves not at all animated by his presence; if he was disappointed with us, we were tenfold more so in him. We saw nothing that looked like spirit. He never appeared with cheerfulness or vigour to animate us. Our men began to despise him; some asked if he could speak ... I am sure the figure he made dejected us; and, had he sent us but five thousand men of good troops, and never come himself among us, we had done other things than we have now done.

The Pretender had not got five thousand good troops at his disposal. He had to make the best of Mar's men and they of him. On 6 January 1716, he duly entered Dundee as the rightful King of Great Britain, and on 9 January he proceeded to Perth. His coronation was ordained for 23 January at the historic palace of Scone, but it never took place. Indeed, the whole of the Pretender's brief sojourn in his kingdom had an air of unreality. Shirley's lines 'The glories of our blood and state, Are shadows, not substantial things' might have been written for the Pretender's Scottish venture. Although it is debatable whether Shirley's next line – 'There is no armour against fate' – was wholly applicable to James Francis Edward. He could have taken better measures to help fate along.

The Duke of Argyle, the distinguished Scottish soldier who led the forces of George I in Scotland. He is seen here in a painting by the Scottish portraitist William Aikman.

'Nous reculons pour mieux sauter'

By the end of January, Argyle's forces had finally been strengthened and they left Stirling to march on Perth. Thereupon the Pretender decided that fate was altogether too much for him. On 4 February, just over six weeks from the day he had landed, he left Scotland and re-embarked for France. Until the last minute, he continued to expect French aid to arrive but when it became evident that nothing was forthcoming from that quarter, he came to the conclusion he must go. He said he left despairingly but to save the Stuart cause for the future – *'Nous reculons pour mieux sauter.'* He said he had to leave because the enemy force was twice as strong as his, but this was not true. Argyle's force, if strengthened, did not begin to outnumber the potential Scottish Jacobite army (although the latter was short of arms). Argyle himself remained gloomy about the Hanoverian prospects and with apparent reason. Much of Scotland was still in the Pretender's hands and would have rallied to vibrant, decisive leadership. Moreover, Argyle could not believe that Mar was as disastrously incompetent as in fact he was. Finally he did not appreciate that the Pretender himself possessed neither powers of leadership nor the ability to recognise or utilise those who had such qualities.

The Jacobite rising was, in effect, defeated as much by its own incompetence and disorganisation as by the English or loyalist Scottish counter-measures. It has been rightly said that the Stuarts represented an antiquated system, that the divine right of kings and all it entailed was doomed. It has been further suggested that the English and loyalist Scots recognised that the future lay with Parliamentary monarchy. Perhaps some of them did, but the majority were surely not as prescient, and absolute monarchy continued to hold sway in much of Europe for a further century. The desire for stability and the Pretender's inability to evoke enthusiasm played as large a part in his defeat as noble concepts of Parliamentary democracy.

On his ignominious return to France, the Pretender was forced to leave his Court at St Germain. His failure had convinced the French Regent that reconciliation with the Hanoverian dynasty was the course to follow. He therefore no longer wanted a claimant to the English throne on his doorstep. James Francis Edward found asylum at Avignon for a time but later, as an alliance between England and France was negotiated, he was forced out of France and had to cross into Italy, further yet and further from his true kingdom.

Back in Scotland, early in 1716, the remnants of the Jacobite army, unaware that their King had left their shores, were still expecting to fight Argyle. But once the news spread that the Pretender had gone, the clansmen melted away. Argyle was able to re-take the pro-Jacobite cities without a fight. At the end of February the more forceful Cadogan ousted Argyle from command in Scotland and set about the task of pacifying the country. Compared with what happened after the 1745 rebellion, the pacification was mild. There was some burning and looting, the property of noble Jacobite rebels was confiscated, Jacobites were arrested, though many fled into the hills and Cadogan did not bother to give chase. None was hanged and after several months many of the prisoners were allowed out of the overcrowded gaols. Eighteen months later, a general amnesty was granted by Act of Parliament to the former rebels.

The only exception to the amnesty was the famous Rob Roy McGregor. His exploits during the actual rebellion were very much a personal side-show and had no effect whatsoever on its course. The McGregor expedition to Loch Lomond was in fact a disaster, easily repulsed by the stalwart, loyalist citizens of Paisley and Dumbarton. The exemption from the amnesty was not surprising either, as Rob Roy's McGregors had been outlaws for a century. Thus the guerilla warfare which they carried on after the rebellion was an extension of their old outlaw activities. Rob Roy's immortality as a Scottish Robin Hood owes more to the genius of Sir Walter Scott's pen than to reality.

The King's ministers behaved extremely sensibly towards Scotland and its rebels after the 1715 rising. In an era in which moderation towards treason was not the keynote, and severe forms of punishment for all felonies and misdemeanours were common, their lack of vengeful measures was the more remarkable. For the time being, they were rewarded for their moderation. Scotland became calm and unrebellious.

The attitude towards the English lords who had risen in rebellion and towards the Anglo-Scots invasion force defeated at Preston, was more severe. But on the whole, allowing for the fierce standards of the time, the keynote was again surprising moderation. A couple of dozen officers captured at Preston were sentenced to death. A random example was made of the troops, an unfortunate one in twenty being sentenced to transportation as convicts to the West Indies. Seven noble lords were brought to London to be tried before their peers. Six of them – Lords Widdrington and Nairn, Viscount Kenmure, and the Earls of Derwentwater, Carnwath and Nithsdale – were tried in a London suffering from an extreme winter. The Thames had frozen over, and the ice was sufficiently thick to allow a fair to be set up on its surface, for oxen to be roasted thereon, and to encourage the Duke of Marlborough and the Prince of Wales to venture out for an icy walk.

All six of the noblemen were sentenced to the customary horrible death for the high treason of which they had been found guilty – 'you must be hanged by the neck but not until you are dead; for you must be cut down alive, then your bowels must be taken out, and burnt before your faces; then your heads must be severed from your bodies, and your bodies divided each into four quarters; and these must be at the king's disposal'. In practice, this hideous sentence of hanging, drawing and quartering was not effected for peers of the realm, but was reduced to straightforward beheading. In the event, only two of the prisoners, Viscount Kenmure and the Earl of Derwentwater, were actually executed. Both died gallantly, Derwentwater proclaiming his Catholic faith and commending his soul to God, Kenmure expressing sorrow 'that I did not provide myself with a black suit, that I might have died more decently'. The executions of three of the other lords were for various reasons postponed, and each was eventually pardoned. The sentences produced one dramatic escape which, like the story of Rob Roy, was to be seized upon by future writers and take its place in the romantic annals of British history.

The sixth prisoner was Lord Nithsdale, incarcerated in the Tower of London awaiting execution along with his fellow nobles. Nithsdale had an enterprising, determined, strong-minded wife, Winifred. First she tried to plead for her husband's life with the King. But George treated her much as he had treated Sophia Dorothea, with a boorish lack of grace. In a letter to her sister, Winifred Nithsdale described the scene thus:

A clear Stage and no Favour.

'I threw myself at his feet, and told him in French that I was the unfortunate Countess of Nithsdale, that he might not pretend to be ignorant of my person. . . . I caught hold of his skirt. . . . He endeavoured to escape out of my hands . . . he dragged me upon my knees from the middle of the room to the very door . . . the petition, which I had endeavoured to thrust into his pocket, fell down in the scuffle.' If one is being kind to George one could say that it was the sheer embarrassment of a shy man who hated scenes which caused his behaviour, rather than callousness. He was reported as acting more graciously towards Lady Derwentwater who had similarly gone down on her knees before him to beg for her husband's life. George was supposed to have said to Lady Derwentwater's less persistent appeal, 'I sincerely regret, Madam, to see you in this distressing position.'

In any case, Lady Nithsdale was not daunted by her experience in the drawing room of the King's apartments. Next she presented a petition to the House of Lords, pleading for clemency. When that failed, she evolved the plan which captured the imagination of future authors – to smuggle her

The Earl of Derwentwater and Viscount Kenmure, two of the lords executed for their part in the 1715 uprising.

105

Two contemporary woodcuts:
ABOVE The procession to the Tower
of the defeated Scottish rebels.
BELOW Their death by fire.

husband out of the Tower disguised as a woman. The night before his execution, accompanied by two female friends, she visited her husband at the Tower. All were wearing voluminous cloaks which enveloped a great many props. Lady Nithsdale made certain that there was considerable to-ing and fro-ing up and down the stairs from the condemned man's cell, so that the guards would be confused as to how many ladies had actually left the precincts. While these guards imagined that they were attending on distraught women taking their leave of a doomed man, Lady Nithsdale was busy, working on her husband's appearance. In her own words,

> I painted his face white, and his cheeks with rouge, to hide his long beard, which he had not had time to shave. ... When I had almost finished dressing my lord in all his petticoats, I perceived it was growing dark, and was afraid the light of the candles might betray us. ... I went out leading him by the hand, and he held his handkerchief to his eyes. ... The guards opened the door, and I went downstairs with him. ... As soon as he had cleared the door, I made him walk before me, for fear the sentinels should take notice of his walk. ...

But the sentinels did not notice the Earl of Nithsdale's manly gait, and he reached the exit. Lady Nithsdale herself returned to the cell and talked to her husband 'as if he had really been present, and answered my own questions in my lord's voice as nearly as I could imitate it'. Then she too left the cell. Both guards and sentinels failed to notice that three women had entered the Tower but four had left.

Nithsdale went into hiding but was quickly smuggled out of the country, with the unwitting connivance of the Venetian ambassador. In Italy, his wife joined him and they spent the rest of their lives there. News of the escape was the talk of London for weeks. Some were delighted, others horrified, according to where their political sympathies lay. George's reaction is more difficult to gauge. One source claimed that 'he flew into an excess of passion, and said he was betrayed', another that he remarked laconically, 'It is the best thing that a man in his situation could have done.' The former remark sounds the more probable, as George was not noted for his pithy, ironic phrases whereas he was known for his tendency to feel betrayed. George had not displayed tact or compassion when Nithsdale's fellow

Jacobite lords were executed. On the night of their execution he attended a ball, an attendance which was not viewed kindly even in anti-Jacobite, pro-Hanoverian circles. Derwentwater and Kenmure had been noblemen, if misguided – and who had not been 'misguided' in an era of shifting allegiance? It was felt that the King might have shown greater sensitivity.

The seventh nobleman brought to London and incarcerated in the Tower was Lord Wintoun. By a series of ingenious delaying tactics he managed to postpone his trial until three months after those of his fellow Jacobites. When finally brought to trial, Wintoun stretched the proceedings to a full three days, though there were some who said his ingeniousness was based on insanity rather than cleverness. Whether insane, eccentric or coolly brilliant, Wintoun also managed to avoid the death sentence duly passed upon him. Like his fellow nobleman, the Earl of Nithsdale, he too escaped from the Tower of London and succeeded in reaching the Continent. As his escape was effected by the simple means of sawing through the bars of his cell, rather than the dramatic method of leaving the Tower disguised as a woman, it has not passed into the history books or the realms of literature.

By mid-1716, immediate fears of a Jacobite rebellion had evaporated. Both England and Scotland relaxed into tranquillity, assisted by the moderation shown by the Whigs in power. It is easy to say now that the Whigs could afford to be generous and tolerant. The rebellion had brought to the surface the Jacobite supporters who had either fled the country or had their wings clipped by imprisonment or removal from office. It had demonstrated that there was no overwhelming demand for a Stuart restoration. Therefore, overall, it had immeasurably strengthened the Whig/Hanoverian position. But there remained an undertow of support for the Stuarts which could have become a mainstream again if George I or the Whigs had behaved in too unpopular a manner or failed to keep the economy booming. On the Continent there were many rulers and politicians willing to utilise the Stuarts against England if it suited their purpose. Above all, James Francis Edward was alive and well, and as long as he was, he – and his children – would be the focal point for Stuart hopes and intrigues. In 1716, it was no more obvious to the Whigs than it

A Victorian representation of the much romanticised escape of Lord Nithsdale from the Tower, planned by his wife. Dressed in women's clothing, he passed by the sentinels without being recognised.

Frost Fair on the River

LONDON

Temple   Stairs

E

G   B   F   G

A

A

C   D   B

H   Thames

Buttons or Buckles

I

A *Goldsmiths*. B *Turners*. C *ye Rowling Press Printers*. D *ye comon Pr*
F *Tunbridge Ware*. G *Toyshops*. H *Flying Coaches*. I *Gameing Table*

Printed on the Thames Ian   17 15/16

The Frost Fair held on the River
Thames when it was frozen over
during the winter of 1715/16. It was

at this time that the rebels were
brought to London for
punishment.

110

had been to Bolingbroke in 1715 that the Stuart cause was doomed. The Whig moderation in the aftermath of the rebellion was doubly sensible and sagacious.

George's reactions to the Stuart rising were not well-documented. That uncommunicative monarch kept his thoughts to himself. But one of his ministers said that if James Francis Edward had succeeded and had marched on London, George would never have surrendered but would have gone down fighting. At first glance, this seems an odd assessment. George's lack of enthusiasm for England was well-known. Would not the approach of the Pretender have provided him with an excellent opportunity to pack his bags and happily return to Hanover, accompanied by all his playfellows, male and female? On second thoughts, George had been a soldier and nobody cast doubts on his personal courage. Having been called to the English throne by Parliament and the people, he might have defended the crown to the death.

5 The Hanoverians

Vultures Settle In 1716-17

WITH THE JACOBITES SUBDUED and the Whigs strengthened, George and his Hanoverian courtiers were able to return their attention to establishing themselves in England temporarily at least, for George was soon off back to Hanover. Of the actual country in which they so surprisingly found themselves in such privileged positions, few of the Hanoverians saw anything. They may have been an acquisitive group but they were not inquisitive. What went on outside the environs of the Court was unknown to them.

England in the second decade of the eighteenth century had a population of about six million (accurate estimates are impossible to give, as there was then no census. Although parishes had been required to keep records since Tudor times there was no official registration of births, marriages or deaths). Of these six million people, some seven hundred thousand lived in London. However, the capital never dominated English life to the extent that Paris dominated France. This can be accounted for by many reasons. Traditional centres of industries such as wool and silk manufacture, and ports such as Bristol, guarded their independence jealously. As their power waned, new industrial centres rose in the north and Midlands to attract attention from London. The English art of compromise, for tacit understandings, had led to the minimum of laws and to a very loose, fluid system. The lack of bureaucracy meant that less focus was put on the capital. People in the shires and cities and boroughs continued to lead their own lives, little directed from London. Again in England the long fight between King and Parliament had meant that the aristocracy and country gentlemen had played a larger part in government than in most European countries. The gentry spent as much time at home as in London which again dispersed the spheres of power and influence.

Basically, England was still an agricultural country, though more and more people were beginning to drift towards the towns. The countryside was mostly open and unhedged. It was not until later in the eighteenth century, with the coming of the Enclosure Acts, that the now familiar landscape of small fields and neat hedges took shape. The chief industry remained the woollen one, centred on East Anglia and the south-west, with some activity in the West Riding of Yorkshire. Tin was mined

PREVIOUS PAGES Covent Garden during the reign of George 1, painted by the Flemish artist Jacob van Aken.

114

A print showing ploughs used at the beginning of the eighteenth century. England's economy was still basically rural at this time.

in Cornwall, lead in Derbyshire, but the old-established iron industry was in decline because of the shortage of wood fuel. Coal was only just beginning to assume importance as a means of providing heat and power. Each area had its own individuality and traditions, influenced by the dominating local town.

There was a number of fair-sized towns, most of them still in the southern half of the country. The north was on the whole regarded as being inhabited by rude barbarians into whose areas it was well not to venture unless one had one's estates there or necessity dictated the journey. Scotland was as much beyond the pale as Ireland. The few English travellers who had to set foot there were appalled by everything they saw, including the scenery. The romantic revival had yet to occur and the glens, the lochs and the mountains were viewed with distaste. One English traveller considered the Highlands frightful, 'most disagreeable of all when the heath is in bloom'. Ireland retained her nominal Parliament in Dublin, with the King as head of state and with England holding powers of veto and responsible for foreign and other important affairs. In the early eighteenth century, Ireland was in a period of quiescence, so few Englishmen bothered about her unless they were sent there in a political capacity, which usually meant in semi-disgrace. Wales was regarded as an integral part of England and its inhabitants were viewed in much the same manner as north countrymen, as rude, ignorant barbarians.

One of the reasons people travelled so little was the appalling state of the few roads that existed, particularly in the winter months. A traveller in the Midlands wrote, 'the road was so full of holes and quick sands I durst not venture', and again, 'very deep bad roads ... full of sloughs, clay deep way, that I was near 11 hours in going but 25 mile'. Most villages were therefore self-contained units, operating on a semi-feudal system with the Lord of the Manor or squire holding authority – 'God bless the squire and his relations Who keep us in our proper stations.' The standard of village life and the happiness of the 'stations' was greatly dependent on whether the squire was good or bad, on whether he felt a sense of responsibility towards his inferiors. However, the villagers retained a measure of independence. Ancient Common Law rights enabled them to grow food on their own strip of land, to graze their cattle on the common land, to gather brushwood or turf from the waste-land for fuel and to collect the gleanings from the community harvest which helped bread supplies during the winter months. On the whole, food supplies were adequate, as the population had not yet outstripped England's capacity to feed herself.

There was political consciousness among the populace, more so than in the majority of European countries. 'The mob' was easily capable of being roused in England, and since the 'Glorious Revolution' it had possessed the right to petition the monarch on the subject of its grievances, a legal right not generally accorded in Europe. It was Bolingbroke who said, 'The Constitution of England is the business of every Englishman.' But, by and large, the majority of Englishmen did not

'God bless the squire and his relations Who keep us in our proper stations'

116

consider it their particular business. Government was a matter best left to the King and their masters – a view the King and their masters encouraged them to hold. In the rural areas, the education which could have heightened political consciousness and general awareness, was sadly lacking. But overall, the spread of education for the poor was again wider than in most European countries. There were the endowed grammar schools, the Dissenters had their own schools (among the best of the time) and the Society for Promoting Christian Knowledge was establishing charity schools.

Again, the majority of these schools were in the towns, and England remained an agricultural country. Despite the hard core of a literate, thinking, politically-conscious lower class, there was a general acceptance of the *status quo*. At the top of the pyramid was the aristocracy, underneath there were the gentry in the country and the merchants in the towns, then there was a growing stratum of the middle class, with the village labourers in the country and the town poor at the bottom. But the idea that traditional class barriers could or should be broken, that everybody was entitled to a fair share of the riches of the country, had not rooted, which is not to say it had not been mooted: the Levellers and other groups in the Cromwellian era had tried their hands at idealistic forms of communism.

If there was generally a placid acceptance of the established system, to most European visitors it appeared that England was a country in which the populace had already achieved a high degree of freedom. To the Hanoverians, accustomed to the despotism of their state, it was a country with an upper class inclined not to show due deference to their monarch, surmounting an unruly populace which it barely controlled. Another factor commented upon by visiting Europeans was the British (basically English) sense of superiority. A French observer wrote, 'I do not think there is a people more prejudiced in its own favour than the British people, and they allow this to appear in their talk and manners. They look on foreigners in general with contempt and think nothing is as well done elsewhere as in their own country.' One set of foreigners regarded with a high degree of contempt was the Hanoverians, but if they ensured that the atmosphere of prosperity continued, the contempt would be mingled with tolerance. Of the generally

FOLLOWING PAGES
Painting around 1750, Canaletto produced many views of London. Here he shows Whitehall and the Privy Gardens.

prosperous atmosphere, Daniel Defoe wrote, 'They eat well and they drink well. ... Even those we call poor people, journeymen, working and pains-taking people do thus; they lye warm, live in plenty, work hard and know no want.' These observations, written to boost Robert Walpole's leadership, should be taken with a leavening of scepticism. By no means everybody ate well, lay warm or lived in plenty, and some of the poorest of the poor were in London.

The capital, if not dominating English life, was the centre of power and the greatest activity. After the Great Fire of 1666, there had been a rash of building. St James's, Soho and Golden Squares had been built since the fire, while Hanover – named in honour of the King – and Cavendish Squares were in the process of being constructed. But there was not a vestige of planning in the fast-growing capital, it just expanded like a piece of elastic. (Sir Christopher Wren had drawn up detailed plans to rebuild London but, alas, they were not implemented.) The division between East and West Ends was becoming more apparent. The plague which had preceeded the Great Fire had sent the nobility and rich merchants hurrying away from the City. The direction they had naturally taken had been westwards, rather than eastwards towards the marshes of the Thames. The old industries and commercial life tended to remain in the City, which became the East End, while the West End – where the Court was at St James's – became more the habitat of the wealthy. Areas such as Spitalfields, long the home of the weavers, had been given a fresh impetus by the influx of Huguenot refugees who fled from France in 1685 when Louis XIV revoked the Edict of Nantes. (This Edict of Henri of Navarre's had previously granted civil and religious liberties to French Protestants.) These areas increasingly became the domain of 'the industrious classes' or the very poor. Some of the most filthy slums already festered round Shoreditch in the East End, but they existed in the West End too, frequently cheek by jowl with the gracious new architecture. The area round Drury Lane was a notorious warren of brothels, pickpockets, highwaymen and the dregs of eighteenth-century society. Lady Mary Wortley Montagu wrote of 'the loathsome cripples' who infested every part of the town.

The Thames remained London's main artery, and it was

navigable as far up as Lechlade. But in the City itself there was still only one bridge – the old London Bridge with its shops and houses – linking it to the South Bank. Dominating the ever-sprawling capital – with its stinking alleyways, its gracious squares, its huddled tenements, its elegant coffee houses, its dark warehouses and bright theatres – was Sir Christopher Wren's noble edifice, St Paul's Cathedral. Its vast dome towered over the city, and when the sun shone, its new Portland stone glistened.

Everywhere in London, life was cheap. The sanctity of

A London street-pedlar drawn by Marcellus Laroon for a series of prints called 'The Cries of London'.

FOLLOWING PAGES Here Canaletto illustrates how the great dome of St Paul's dominated the city during the Hanoverian period.

The Churches of London

The reign of George I saw the construction of a
number of the most famous churches in central
London under an Act which provided for the
building of fifty new churches. Among the leading
architects were Nicholas Hawksmoor and the
Scottish-born James Gibbs. Both developed
the English Baroque style which had been
introduced by Sir Christopher Wren during the
preceding century.

124

BELOW St Mary-le-Strand, James Gibbs's masterpiece.
LEFT Hawksmoor's statue of St George from the spire of St George's, Bloomsbury, an idealised representation of George I.
BELOW LEFT The noble portico of Hawksmoor's Christchurch, Spitalfields, built in 1721.
RIGHT In 1720 Gibbs rebuilt the old church of St Martin's-in-the-Fields, combining a classical portico with a steeple.

individual life might be a Western Christian concept but it was not one which had penetrated deeply in the early half of the eighteenth century. It was expected that smallpox and other diseases would carry off a fair percentage of the population every year. It was expected that out of every hundred children born, a further good percentage would die in infancy. In living memory, plague and fire had drastically reduced the population and destroyed property. With nature so uncaring and natural disaster so prevalent, who but a fool would set a high value on an individual's life? Thus there was the strong strain of what appears to later generations as callousness.

Cock-fighting, bear-baiting and prize fighting – in which the human contestants literally smashed each other to pulp – were immensely popular with all sectors of society. Visits to Bedlam, to watch the antics of the insane, were equally popular forms of entertainment. Public whippings and stonings and pilloryings were commonplace, while public executions were the signal for a general holiday and merrymaking. In a sense all these activities were a release from the harshness and unpredictability of everyday life; while in the absence of too many laws, of a police force or a large standing army, the public punishments reminded the populace what could happen to them if they did not behave themselves.

Gambling was another early eighteenth-century obsession in all walks of life, in middle- and upper-class coffee houses as much as lower-class taverns. Again, it was a reaction against the impervious, random face of nature. Here today, gone to-morrow, was only too true a saying. The urge to gamble on being here tomorrow, to spit in the face of providence, was widespread. But as much as gracious architecture existed side by side with hideous slums in the towns, as vast houses and estates spread among the comparative poverty of the villages, so high sensibility, aesthetic appreciation, a genuine love of the arts and sciences went hand in hand with the callousness and brutality.

Queen Anne's reign had witnessed a flowering of English, and Anglo-Irish, literature. Alexander Pope, Dean Swift, Addison, Steele and John Gay had emerged, although curiously they were not considered particularly highly at the time, or for several decades afterwards. In the fields of mathematics, astronomy and philosophy one of the greatest and nicest men of his, or any other, age – Sir Isaac Newton – still flourished. His great fundamental work lay behind him – on the composition of light, on geometry and the differential calculus, on the laws of dynamics and the entwined subject for which he is best remembered, the theory of gravity. Incidentally, Newton's work on the first rules of calculus was published slightly after Gottfried Wilhelm Leibnitz's on the same subject, and which of the two eminent mathematicians had done the more fundamental work led to a major and prolonged dispute. There is the story that when George was congratulated on becoming King of England he replied, 'Rather congratulate me on having Newton for a subject in one country, and Leibnitz in the other.' It sounds an unlikely story. Both the phrasing and the thought seem too original for the dull, uncommunicative George. However, once in England, George's lack of interest meant that the flower of the country continued to blossom, with fairly untrammelled freedom, on all fronts. On the literary front writers enjoyed themselves denigrating the stupidity, the rapacity, the philistinism of their new Hanoverian King and his courtiers.

George's two mistresses came in for some of the more wicked comments, and by this time Mademoiselle Schulenberg had arrived at the Court of St James's. She and the earlier arrival, Madame Kielmansegge, were dually described as 'ugly old trulls, such as would not find entertainment in the most hospitable hundreds of old Drury'. Individually, Mademoiselle Schulenberg was described as long and emaciated, tall, lean and ugly, 'by no means an inviting object'. Lady Mary Wortley Montagu said, 'She was duller than the King, and consequently did not find out that he was so.' There was complete agreement that she was totally avaricious. Robert Walpole said, 'She would have sold the King's honour for a shilling advance to the best bidder', and he was an expert on human greed.

The younger Madame Kielmansegge earned slightly kinder treatment. Lady Mary Wortley Montagu paid her a somewhat back-handed compliment by writing, 'She had greater vivacity in conversation than ever I knew in a German of either sex.' Nonetheless, Madame Kielmansegge's figure was described as enormous, corpulent or, at the best, ample. Horace Walpole

'Ugly old trulls, such as would not find entertainment in the most hospitable hundreds of old Drury'

painted a graphic pen portrait of her, 'Two fierce black eyes, large and rolling, beneath two lofty arched eye-brows. Two acres of cheeks spread with crimson, an ocean of neck that overflowed and was not distinguished from the lower part of her body, and no part restrained by stays ... the mob of London were highly diverted at the importation of so uncommon a seraglio!' Caroline of Anspach, the Princess of Wales, said of Madame Kielmansegge 'She never stuck a pin into her gown without design', and another commentator recorded that 'her character for rapacity was not inferior' to that of Mademoiselle Schulenberg. For obvious reasons of size, the two royal mistresses were referred to as 'the Maypole and the Elephant'.

Lady Mary Wortley Montagu also recorded her overall impression of the Hanoverian ladies of the Court: 'All the women have literally rosy cheeks, snowy foreheads and bosoms, jet eye-brows and scarlet lips, to which they generally add coal-black hair. These perfections never leave them till the hour of their death, and they have a very fine effect by candle-light. ... They resemble one another as much as Mrs Salmon's [waxwork] court of Great Britain, and are in as much danger of melting away by too near approaching the fire.'

The amount of power and influence wielded by Mesdames Kielmansegge and Schulenberg and the other Hanoverians was initially vast. It was vast because the King was still the real ruler of England. Despite the limitations on royal power imposed by the Act of Settlement, the King had the right to appoint and dismiss ministers. Acts of Parliament or the decision of his ministers (not in the eighteenth century by any means the same thing) had to be sanctioned by him. His veto, if allowed to be applied, was final. In essence, Parliament still regarded its function as ensuring that the King did not rule too despotically and autocratically or fail to take due note of Parliament's wishes and the rights of the propertied classes. A Member of Parliament said picturesquely, 'Our business is to fly in the King's face. We were sent here to fly in the King's face.' Thus, although ultimate power now lay with Parliament, if it chose to exercise it, real day-to-day power remained at the Court centred on the personage of the King.

George was not unaware of his position, nor wholly lacking in interest in his new kingdom and its government, although to

128

Lady Mary Wortley Montagu, the lovely and enterprising wife of the Ambassador to Constantinople, whose prolific output of letters includes thumb-nail sketches of many of her contemporaries, which make witty reading even today.

a degree, having been called by the will of Parliament rather than the will of God, he underestimated the powers he retained. He was not the stupidest monarch who ever sat on the English throne, though again Lady Mary Wortley Montagu was among the many who castigated his stupidity, saying he was 'an honest blockhead ... more properly dull than lazy'. George could be shrewd if occasion demanded. He could certainly be obstinate. He was capable of nursing royal animosity towards those who thwarted him. When his interest was aroused, he could display industry and tenacity, as he had with the re-organisation of the armies of the Upper Rhine and as he usually did when Hanover was the issue. What he possessed was an innately closed, limited mind. He had never particularly wanted to be King of England and nothing about the country, its inhabitants or its peculiar method of government aroused his small stock of enthusiasm. Thus in England he gave the impression of being duller, more stupid and lazy, more generally uninterested than he was.

If the King appeared to display only an intermittent interest in England, quite a bit about the country roused the enthusiasm of his Hanoverian courtiers and ministers, namely the pickings to be had. When George first became King he obviously gave his trust to the people he knew and understood, with whom he felt comfortable and relaxed, the Hanoverians. Thus their power was initially great, and there was a scramble among ambitious English politicians to enlist the support of those who had the King's confidence, Mesdames Kielmansegge and Schulenberg, Jean de Robethon, Barons von Bothmar and Bernstorff. One thing over which the King retained absolute control was patronage. All civil servants were the King's own servants, paid out of his own money (granted by Parliament). All appointments to the royal household were made by him. Many of these appointments had already grown rusty with age, and were in fact sinecures. The rush to snatch them, with the fat salaries for doing nothing, was headlong. Who, initially, for large bribes, influenced the indifferent King in making these appointments? His Hanoverian mistresses, ministers and courtiers, including his two Muslim servants, Mustapha and Mahomet.

The Hanoverian rapacity within this field was undeniable. In the words of a contemporary, 'A flight of hungry Hanoverians like so many famished vultures, fell with keen eyes and bended talons on the fruitful soil of England.' The true-born English courtier, already so conscious of his racial superiority, greatly resented having to go cap in hand to the Hanoverian vultures (although the chauvinistic courtiers might have recalled Daniel Defoe's poem, *The True Born Englishman*, which with immense gusto had traced the mixed mongrel pedigree of 'that heterogenous thing, an Englishman' who was 'from amphibious, ill-born mob begun'). The native courtiers accepted that one bribed one's way to the lucrative posts in the King's service but they hated having to ask Germans – and such grasping and stupid Germans – for the favours. Not unfounded accusations

'A flight of hungry Hanoverians like so many famished vultures'

of gross Hanoverian corruption were hurled about the Court, and spread outwards towards the populace. Undoubtedly the venality and greed of the Hanoverians, Mademoiselle Schulenberg in particular, played its part in the spread of bribery and corruption which became such a dominant feature of eighteenth-century political life.

Because the King retained so much power, politics were obviously entangled with the Court. But if one can arbitrarily disentangle them, on the political level the Whigs solidified the position they had won on George's accession. This was partly because George's lack of interest in England did not extend to re-admitting the Tories to office, partly because the Hanoverians favoured the Whigs, partly because the Tories themselves were in such disarray. They never had a chance to recover from the bitter internal dissensions wrought by Bolingbroke in his last days of office. Moreover, they were tarred with the Jacobite brush, a taint the Whigs did not allow to be purified.

We should clarify what the terms 'Whig' and 'Tory' represented in the early eighteenth century. Any idea that they corresponded to the later Liberal and Conservative parties, or to present-day parties must be dismissed. The concept of a political party, with a set of principles, giving its allegiance to a leader, behaving in a disciplined manner and voting in unity, did not exist. What existed was a loose association of politicians who at a given time might hold the same set of views or, occasionally, principles, but who were more likely to have common self-interest, and whose allegiance could change at any moment, because the allegiance went to the men who in their spheres wielded vast power and patronage. It went to the heads of the great aristocratic families of England, the Pelhams, the Cavendishes, the Stanhopes, the Cecils and others. What party politics really meant in the eighteenth century was the fight for power between the great families. What the Hanoverians thought they could be, and to a degree were in their early days, was another power block, rivalling the great Houses.

The terms Whig and Tory did exist. Contemporaries spoke of the Whigs or Tories being in office. The limited electorate, not all of whom could be bribed all of the time, voted for a Whig or Tory candidate. Pamphlets denigrating each faction abounded. So what did they represent? Roughly, the Tories

Low Life in London

The 1720s saw the emergence of William Hogarth, England's first great caricaturist, whose lively interpretations of life among all classes of eighteenth-century society have rarely been equalled by any artist since. Here is a selection of his works.

LEFT Hogarth's representation of a cockfight emphasises the brutality of this sport which, like bear-baiting and prize-fighting, appealed to all groups of society.

LEFT An engraving of tipplers in a tavern described by Hogarth as 'a modern midnight conversation'.
RIGHT 'The Sleeping Congregation', one of Hogarth's earliest satirical works.
BELOW Southwark Fair in 1731. On the right is the stand of Mr James Figgs, who was the first professional British pugilist. His trade card described him as the 'Oxonian Professor' of fisticuffs!

represented the rights of the King, the Constitution, the Church of England and the gentry as by law and custom established, with more emphasis on the rights of the King, the Church and the gentry than on Parliament's. Roughly, the Whigs stood for the greater rights of Parliament, the mercantile classes, the voice of dissent and nonconformity, religious and otherwise. However blurred and imprecise these dividing lines frequently were in practice, the existence of these two embryonic parties was a peculiarly English institution. Their growth, slow and corrupt as it was in the eighteenth century, prevented either the King or any particular faction in Parliament gaining too great power. The bitterly-contested elections which arose as a result of the party spirit stimulated the existing interest in politics. Eighteenth-century elections were rather like the University Boat Race: even if you had no vote, as even if you never set foot in Oxford or Cambridge, your partisan feelings could be stimulated and interest widened.

From George's accession in 1714 until the middle of 1716, the Whigs closed ranks in the face of the Jacobite threat. Once this had dissipated, though on the surface they remained a coherent body, behind the scenes the personal jealousies and ambitions reared their heads. It was in these years that Barons von Bothmar and Bernstorff wielded their greatest power, for they had the King's confidence. It was also in this period that Jean de Robethon earned his reputation as the master of slimy intrigue, though he was not the only person crawling in the slime. He was joined by a number of English politicians.

The leading contenders for supreme power were Townshend supported by his brother-in-law Walpole, and Stanhope. They were joined by another contender, Charles Spencer, Earl of Sunderland, an aristocrat of great personal charm and wit, married to a daughter of the Marlboroughs (though they were not overfond of him and had failed to assist his career). He was exceedingly ambitious and possessed many attributes for success, including intelligence. He was a brilliant, cool-headed intriguer but he was marred by outbursts of passion when crossed and an inability to compromise. This arose basically because of his high estimation of his own abilities, of the undoubted rights due to a man of his birth and breeding. It made him detest Townshend and Walpole, his social inferiors.

On George's accession, Sunderland – to his intense astonishment – was fobbed off with the Lord Lieutenancy of Ireland (a post engineered by Townshend, who rightly saw him as a leading rival, with Hanoverian connivance). But Sunderland was soon back at Court. His obvious qualities, assisted by the steady flattery and bribery of Mademoiselle Schulenberg, Bothmar and Robethon, quickly had him in the ministry again. Then the fight for power, which Walpole nicely described as 'the heats and divisions betwixt the King's servants', really warmed up. The fight was complicated, and from Sunderland's angle assisted, by George's decision to return to Hanover for a visit.

By July 1716, George had been absent from his beloved homeland for the best part of two years. He could not bear to be parted from the sights and sounds of his country and people any longer. He could say the Stuart threat had been defeated, and he had the reasonable excuse that his Hanoverian affairs needed attention. Officially, according to the Act of Settlement, he could not leave England without the consent of Parliament but in the event Parliament allowed him to go without difficulty. But there was one problem – who should be acting head of state in the King's absence? The only candidate was the heir-apparent, George, Prince of Wales, and the obvious step was to appoint him Regent. But George I was not interested in obvious steps when they concerned his son.

It is doubtful that George ever liked his only son, although he did like his daughter, even if she was named Sophia Dorothea after her mother. It was said that she was the only human being for whom he ever cared. Once he wrote to the younger Sophia Dorothea assuring her he would always love her tenderly, a startling declaration for the reticent George. His feelings towards his son were quite different. The Prince of Wales was nine years old when his mother was imprisoned in Ahlden Castle, old enough to have clear memories of her and defined emotions towards her. The emotions were affectionate. He always carried his mother's portrait on him, if hidden, and one of his first actions on becoming King was to place her portrait in a prominent position for all to see. There were also touching if doubtful stories that as an adolescent he had attempted to swim the moat at Ahlden to gain access to the castle and his

'The heats and divisions betwixt the King's servants'

135

'Cette diablesse Madame la Princesse'

mother. But Prince George had inherited many of his father's characteristics, he too was obstinate and not very clever. However, he was not as shy or gauche in company as his father; he liked society and he enjoyed more worldly associates and entertainments. He also had a clever wife, Caroline of Anspach, whom he respected and, in the Guelph tradition of infidelity, loved. There were obvious and endless clashes of temperament between the two Georges, occasioned on the one hand by the similar obstinacy and limited intellect, on the other by the father's reserved dullness and the son's more lively interests. In the background was the formidable Caroline whom George I, with his dislike of clever women, called *'cette diablesse Madame la Princesse'* (though later he entertained a grudging respect for her).

When the question arose of appointing his son Regent, George immediately and firmly refused. Undoubtedly, part of the reaction was caused by sheer bloody-mindedness, the 'something' in the Guelph blood which could not bear to see its close relatives having anything their own way. But there was an element of sound political sense in George's reaction, too. This was the element his predecessor Anne had recognised so clearly when she refused to have him or his mother Sophia in England during her life-time. An heir to the throne resident in the country during the monarch's life-time was an obvious focus for all the discontented politicians, all those who for whatever reason disliked the monarch, all those who might plot or plan a rebellion. Despite the mutual ill-feeling, the Prince of Wales had not demonstrated any propensity towards rebellion, but he was resident in England. His father had no intention of leaving him there, fully empowered to act as Regent.

In the end, the impasse was broken by a typically English compromise. The title 'Guardian of the Realm', dating back to the days of the Black Prince, was revived. It carried with it no such powers as that of Regent, which kept the King happy, but was a high-sounding title which kept the Prince of Wales reasonably happy. Thus George set off for Hanover, accompanied by most of his own courtiers and by Stanhope. In Hanover he was received with rapture. The population poured into the beflagged streets, and George responded to his subjects' joy with more enthusiasm than he had shown in the last two years. It was said he was so happy that 'he seemed to have forgot the accident that happened to him and his family on 1st August, 1714'.

While Stanhope went with the King to Hanover, Townshend, as the senior Secretary of State, stayed in London. Townshend and Walpole had faith in the bluff, hearty Stanhope whom they thought was their friend and ally. They were slightly alarmed when their known enemy, Sunderland, suddenly turned up in Hanover but their alarm was tempered by the belief that Stanhope would watch over their interests. Sunderland had rightly come to the conclusion that the seat of intrigue that could lead to power rested where the King currently was. Consequently he pleaded ill-health, and obtained the King's permission to take the waters at Aix-les-Bains. But once out of the country, he changed his destination and made tracks for the political seas of Hanover. There he found the currents conducive to ousting Townshend and Walpole from power.

In the first place Mademoiselle Schulenberg was furious with Townshend. She had wanted to become an English duchess but Townshend, in whose hands the sanction lay, had unwisely granted her only an inferior Irish title, Duchess of Munster. Consequently she was out for his, and his ally Walpole's, blood; as Walpole wrote, she was filled 'with a more than ordinary zeal and resentment against us'. She was not the only Hanoverian thirsting for their downfall. Bernstorff, Bothmar and Jean de Robethon, who had all formerly supported Townshend and Walpole, had decided the Englishmen were becoming too powerful and that a change of Whig leadership, engineered by them, might prove profitable. As Walpole again wrote, 'I fear old Bernstorff has given into these matters [of intrigue] more than we are willing to believe' and 'Robethon's impertinence is so notorious, that we must depend upon it he does all the mischief he possibly can.'

Despite being well aware that the Hanoverians were now against them, and that Sunderland had always been against them, Townshend and Walpole pinned their faith on Stanhope. But Stanhope, egged on by Sunderland's gossip about what was supposed to be happening in London, had decided that Townshend and Walpole were about to stick a knife in his back, and that he must act first. But even with Hanoverian support, persuading the King to agree to dismiss Townshend was not at all easy, for during his two years of office, George had slowly begun to trust and respect Townshend, if not Walpole. Stanhope therefore worked on George's suspicions of his son, and on the complications of British and Hanoverian foreign policy. He told the King that Townshend and Walpole were intriguing behind his back in London with the Prince of Wales. There was not much truth in this, as the Prince of Wales had little liking for Townshend and even less for Walpole. However, Townshend was legitimately insisting that the Prince of Wales should have greater powers during the King's absence, and it was not too difficult for Stanhope to cultivate the suspicions in the King's mind. It was even less difficult to convince the King that Townshend and Walpole were working against Hanoverian interests in the field of foreign affairs.

At the time, the protracted negotiations for what became the Triple Alliance between France, England and the United Dutch Provinces were being held at The Hague. There were delays in signing the treaty. In part, they were due to the fact that English messengers had to travel between London, Hanover and The Hague which prolonged all transactions. They were in larger part due to the ministers in London wanting to ensure that the treaty did not strengthen the French, and that all loose ends were tied up. George himself wanted the treaty signed as quickly as possible. His interest lay in what was happening in Northern Europe where the Tsar Peter had suddenly changed sides and seemed likely to link up with Sweden, thereby threatening the balance of power in the Baltic. If the treaty with France was signed and the threat of a French war removed, Britain could then concentrate her attention on northern affairs to the benefit of Hanover. Apart from the fact that the Triple Alliance was of more importance, neither the ministers in London nor Parliament nor the merchant classes had any desire to get Britain involved in a Baltic war. It was therefore to British interest to play for time, to ensure the satisfactory alliance with France and negate the likelihood of a costly war with Sweden and/or Russia.

Eventually, Stanhope convinced the King that Townshend was working against the true Hanoverian interest. At the end of 1716, George dismissed Townshend from his office as Secretary of State for the Northern Department. He was offered the favourite post for ministers not wholly but partially

Bartholomew Fair in 1721 is depicted on this contemporary fan.

in disgrace, the Lord Lieutenancy of Ireland. However, Stanhope still hoped to retain a united Whig ministry, but with himself and Sunderland at the top instead of Townshend and himself. Consequently, Townshend's ally, Walpole, was not dismissed. Briefly, at the beginning of 1717, with the King's return to London, an appearance of harmony was achieved. But the unity could not be maintained because Stanhope had betrayed Townshend, and it was not long before the latter was dismissed from the Lord Lieutenancy. The next day, Walpole, displaying great loyalty to his brother-in-law, also resigned from the ministry. Walpole's brother later recounted a touching story about the King begging him not to resign, repeatedly pressing the seals of office back into his hand. It does not seem a very likely tale, as George had evinced no warmth towards Walpole. And the people for whom he showed some warmth, the Hanoverians, were only too delighted to see the Norfolk upstart depart.

Thus, at the beginning of 1717, Stanhope and Sunderland had the power for which they had intrigued so heartily. A new ministry was formed, headed by them. But it left a Whig faction in the wilderness, led by the formidable Townshend and the even more formidable Walpole.

Erecting Houses of Office in N. Britain for Strangers & Travellers

A usefall Project merrily advanc'd,
the cheifly by Tom-turdmen countenanc'd,
Design'd to Sweeten the North British Nation,
And put Close Stools, and Bed Pans, out of fashion.

Coal Trade from Newcastle

Some deal in Water, Some in Wind like Fools,
Others in Wood, but we alone in Coals;
From such like Projects, the declining Nation,
May justly fear a fatal inflamation.

Liverpool Fresh-water

This Town does to our Western Islands deal,
And Serves 'em with Malt Liquors, & with Meal,
Both Excellently Good! then how in Nature,
Can People Brew Fine Drink & want Fresh Water.

6

Royal Quarrels and the South Sea Bubble 1717-20

Bastard Children

Love on ye jolly Rakes, and buxome Dames,
A Child is safer than venereal Flames;
Indulge your Senses, with the Sweet offence,
We'll keep your Bastards at a small expence.

Whale Fishery

Whale Fishing, which was once a gainfull Trade,
Is now by cunning Heads, a Bubble made;
For round the Change they only spread their Sailes,
And to catch Gudgeons, bait their Hooks with Whales

An inoffensive way of emptying Houses of Office

Our fragrant Bubble, would the World believe it,
Is to make Humane Dung, smell sweet as Civet:
None sure before us, ever durst presume,
To turn a T — d, into a Rich Perfume.

ROBERT WALPOLE WAS TO BECOME one of England's greatest statesmen and politicians. He was the man who helped create a new style and form of government, and the office of Prime Minister. He was to hold office as the King's first minister for a longer period than anybody who followed him. But in 1717, although few underestimated his abilities and the mastery he had already gained of the House of Commons, equally few would have predicted such a resoundingly brilliant and successful future. In the gambling-obsessed period, large odds could have been obtained against Walpole's fighting his way back to power, let alone the great power he ultimately obtained.

Walpole was born at Houghton in Norfolk in 1676, into a prosperous family of East Anglian squirarchy whose lineage could be traced back to the Norman Conquest. His grandfather and father had been Members of Parliament but he, as a younger son, was destined for the Church. After schooling at Eton, he proceeded to Cambridge but he had been there only two years when his elder brother suddenly died and his father called him home to help manage the family estates. Not long afterwards, in 1700, his father also died and Robert was free to choose his own career and way of life. What he chose to do was to follow in his father's footsteps and enter Parliament.

From the start, he avowed himself a Whig and, on the whole, despite the twists and turns and manœuvres and intrigues, he stayed true to this avowal. Loyalty and consistency were not, in any case, highly prized eighteenth-century attributes, and Walpole can be said to have been more loyal and consistent than most. When he first arrived on the London political scene with his extravagant young wife, Catharine, whom he then loved dearly, he had little to recommend him except his ebullient self-confidence. Class barriers were not as rigid at the end of the seventeenth century as they became during the eighteenth. A man could then break through more easily if he had wit or outrageous talent or high intelligence. But caste was of the utmost importance. Birth and breeding were the passports to success. Although the squirarchy was one of the backbones of England, it did not rank high in the birth and breeding stakes, nor was Walpole closely related to any of the great families. His only contact of any note was with Townshend, an old

family friend. (The closer relationship of brothers-in-law did not occur until 1713 when Townshend finally married Walpole's sister Dorothy, whom he had long cherished.) Townshend, even if he was higher on the social ladder than Walpole and very conscious of the distinction, was only a second generation nobleman and had then obtained little power himself.

The young Walpole was not endowed with a flaring wit or high intelligence, nor was he physically prepossessing, being short and plump (later he became short and gross). But he had a downright, earthy vulgarity and a cast-iron belief in his own capabilities which attracted amused or interested attention in influential Whig circles. He soon proved his brilliance as an administrator, his ability to go to the nub of a problem, to impose order on chaos. He also proved his sound grasp of financial matters, his ability to make knotty economic problems comprehensible to the layman.

Frequently, in his later long, successful career, Walpole showed an amazing lack of awareness of mass sentiment. He had little feeling for the public pulse. But what he possessed to an uncanny degree was an understanding of the individual political animal. Although this might seem an obvious quality among those seeking power, it is rarer than might be imagined. Walpole knew what motivated his fellow-politicians and place-seekers. He knew what would secure their loyalty in the eighteenth-century political arena. His manipulative ability and his knowledge of human weakness was not infallible – he made a serious error about Stanhope – but it was one of his greatest assets. His understanding of human nature, at least in the world of politics, could have been negated had not Walpole also possessed the ability to inspire confidence. He was loathed and reviled by some, but even his bitterest enemies had to admit that Walpole generated an aura of personal reliability. If loyalty and consistency to a party or a cause were not highly rated, a man's individual consistency was. 'To thine own self be true' was not then one of Shakespeare's better-known lines but it had its validity in the whirlpool of eighteenth-century politics. Many men felt that if they placed their trust in Robert Walpole it would not be betrayed, at least not wantonly, viciously, merely for the sake of intrigue. The factor which was to Walpole's

Charles, Earl of Sunderland who, despite his infinitely superior experience in politics in Anne's reign, took second place to Stanhope, aware that the latter held the King's confidence.

Thomas Pelham-Holles, Duke of Newcastle, not noted for his intellect and lacking in calm judgment, widened the rift between the King and the Prince of Wales.

disadvantage as he struggled upwards, his lack of breeding, became more of an advantage as he reached the top. He was always an approachable man and he never lost his joviality. As he assumed more and more power, the down-to-earth manner, the Norfolk vowel sounds – it was said 'he never entirely lost his provincial accent' – his *not* being an aristocrat, made place-seekers feel more comfortable.

In 1717, Walpole was regarded as Townshend's very able assistant. They were a Norfolk partnership, but Townshend was the senior partner. It was thought, particularly by Townshend though he fully appreciated his brother-in-law's abilities, that Walpole would remain in this position. It was ordained by their difference in birth and breeding. What in 1717 was also considered to have been ordained was that both Townshend and Walpole should have received their come-uppance. Townshend might be his brother-in-law's social superior but his blood was not genuinely blue. Two Norfolk upstarts had been justly removed from the position of power they had temporarily seized on George's accession.

The new Whig ministry was led by Stanhope and Sunderland, with Stanhope as the dominant figure. Bereft of Townshend and Walpole and those who followed them into the wilderness, it was not a strong ministry. The appointments to high offices of Joseph Addison and the Duke of Newcastle demonstrated its weakness, how sorely the talents of Townshend and Walpole were missed. Addison was one of England's great essayists, a master of prose, and his political writings in *The Spectator* (founded by himself and his friend Richard Steele) had done much to further the Whig cause, but his talent did not extend to the actual business of politics. As the second Secretary of State, he was a nonentity. The Duke of Newcastle, as Lord Chamberlain, was an even weaker appointment. Newcastle had a great name but he was a young man of strictly limited intelligence, always torn by doubt and liable to panic.

It was Newcastle who precipitated the second and more decisive crisis of relationship between the King and his heir. In 1717, Caroline of Anspach bore the Prince of Wales a second son. At the time, both the King and his heir were in residence at St James's Palace. The Prince of Wales duly invited his father to be godfather to the new prince, and wanted his uncle, the

147

Bishop of Osnabrück, to act as the other godparent. But George insisted that the traditional right of the Lord Chamberlain to be the new-born prince's godfather should be respected. It was not frequently that George took notice of English traditions, and his insistence stemmed from the knowledge that his son would be furious. The Prince of Wales *was* furious, because he hated the Duke of Newcastle, and it was with ill-grace that he accepted his father's command.

After the christening ceremony had been performed, the Prince of Wales's resentment exploded. He advanced on Newcastle, shook his fist vehemently at him and said, 'Rascal, I shall find you out', meaning (it was later gathered) 'I shall find time to be revenged on you.' Unfortunately, neither the Prince's English nor Newcastle's comprehension was good at the best of times. At this particular moment the Prince of Wales was beside himself with rage and Newcastle was shaken to the core by the royal anger. In a panic he decided the Prince had said, 'I shall *fight* you out', and that it was his duty to inform the King that the Prince had threatened his life. Thereupon George became even more furious than his son. A Cabinet meeting was called; ministers were sent to interrogate the Prince of Wales who said the Duke of Newcastle was a liar. Incensed by this slur on his minister, George ordered his son and his wife to be put under house-arrest. Eventually, the King was restrained by Stanhope and Sunderland from taking the drastic step of actually arresting the heir-apparent to the throne or from prolonging the house-arrest. The Prince of Wales, whose mother had already been imprisoned in Ahlden Castle for twenty-three years and therefore knew what his father's anger could entail, became contrite. He had not threatened Newcastle's life but he was willing to admit that his conduct had been unseemly.

The upshot was that the King banished his son and Caroline from St James's Palace and refused to allow them to take their children with them. He said that they could see the children once a week, with his permission, but he would assume responsibility for the princes' and princesses' education. It was a cruel blow, particularly to Caroline, but there was nothing that the Prince of Wales or his wife could do about a decision upheld by a panel of learned judges. It was a further demonstration of the pecular strain of malice in George's character.

'*Rascal, I shall find you out*'

148

Apart from separating the Prince and Princess of Wales from their children, which had its long-term effects on the relationship between the future George II and his sons, the banishment had another effect. The Prince and Princess of Wales set up their own Court at Leicester House. Their Court became a more scintillating place than George's at St James's Palace. This was not a difficult feat considering George's coldness and shyness, his dislike of ceremony, poetry and painting, and the personality of his two less than fascinating mistresses. The rival Court at Leicester House not only shone with a somewhat brighter light, it became the focus for all those politicians, both Whig and Tory, currently out of office. Thus the King himself instituted what Queen Anne had so adroitly avoided, what he had so suspiciously feared – a strong faction centred on the heir-apparent in conflict with the monarch.

It did not become a rebellious faction, but its creation, by the King, had a decided influence on British political life. One of its side-effects was the instituting of the bond which was to be so vital between Walpole and the Prince of Wales when he became George II. This bond did not occur immediately. For a long time the Prince continued to detest the Norfolk squire : on this subject in accord with his father. But the strands of the bond were fashioned during the early Leicester House years, because it was in this period that Walpole established the friendship with Caroline of Anspach which endured until her death. Their *rapport* was immense – it was said they were lovers. Although this was doubtfully true, there was in their friendship the useful element of sexual attraction. Caroline was a handsome woman, with a magnificent pair of breasts which she displayed to maximum advantage on all possible occasions. (Part of her hold over her husband lay in the delights of her flesh.) Like her distinguished grandmother-in-law, the Electress Sophia, she was not as intelligent as she was sometimes made out to be, though Caroline herself fancied the role of blue-stocking. But she had a quick, sharp mind, her knowledge of human frailty and her grasp of politics was not much inferior to Walpole's, and she longed for power as passionately as he did. Walpole had no dislike of attractive, lively women and his excellent political brain told him that the future Queen of England as an ally and confidante would be of inestimable value. However, their friendship was based on more than mutual self-interest, and it endured because they liked and respected each other. With the Walpole relationship established, slowly, cleverly, Caroline began to cultivate her much less intelligent husband's confidence in her chosen minister.

Another even more curious side-effect of the right royal row was that the King ceased to attend Cabinet meetings. The Cabinet had taken shape in the days of Charles II, when he had selected an informal group of Privy Councillors to discuss vital and secret matters of state. By Queen Anne's reign, it had become a feature of government which met regularly, if still informally, and which had certain fixed duties and a certain amount of power (although the notion of a disciplined, coherent Cabinet taking collective decisions lay as far ahead as the disciplined political party system).

Originally George attended Cabinet meetings, as did the Prince of Wales, whose English was better than his father's and who acted as interpreter. After the great quarrel the Prince of Wales was banned from Cabinet meetings and George had nobody to translate directly from English into German. Slowly, George ceased to attend Cabinet meetings which gave his ministers greater freedom to elaborate their own policies. It was Walpole who later took most advantage of the royal absence. Nonetheless, the King still retained his powers. Cabinet measures had to be submitted to him for approval, and if he did not approve, he could veto them. But they were submitted after they had been discussed and only in précis form. The intricacies of what lay behind a particular measure, what its implications might be, were not explained to the King as they would automatically have been had he been present at the Cabinet meetings. Thus, power was imperceptibly taken away from the King and given to the ministers who had to take note of Parliament's wishes from time to time. The concept of Parliamentary monarchy, which stemmed from this greater emphasis on the King's ministers than on the King, began to take shape.

George's ceasing to attend the Cabinet meetings was not entirely prompted by the breach with the Prince of Wales, though the 'something' vicious in the Guelph blood undoubtedly played its part. George spoke and wrote French

B. Ferrers's painting of the Court of Chancery in the reign of George I.

View across the Thames
to Chelsea Hospital,
showing one of Walpole's
houses, painted by
Pieter Tillemans.

'He brushed up
his Latin to
converse with the
first Hanoverian
sovereign'

adequately; so did most of his ministers, some of them extremely well. There is always the story of Horace Walpole's that his father 'brushed up his Latin, to use a phrase of Elizabeth I, to converse with the first Hanoverian sovereign'. The idea of the King and Walpole discussing affairs of state in dog-Latin, 'an instance unparalleled' in British history according to Horace, was more likely an instance of Horace's unparalleled imagination. George and his ministers could have conversed freely and at length in some language, or a mixture of languages, had George so desired. At times, George did so desire and when he needed to, he managed to make his views known clearly. His abstention from the Cabinet was as much prompted by his basic lack of interest in England, of which his failure ever to learn the language was symptomatic.

Robert Walpole's days of influencing the King and controlling the Cabinet had yet to arrive. The years between 1717 and 1720 could not be viewed as high-water marks of his life, apart from the establishment of the vital friendship with Caroline of Anspach. Nor were they happy years for him personally. He and his wife had long been estranged, and though they both continued to live at Walpole's London house in Chelsea their lives were entirely separate. She went her way, he his. When, in 1717, a son was born to Catharine Walpole – the future famous novelist and chronicler of an era, Horace – the rumours that he was not Robert's child but Lord Hervey's were widespread. Later the rumours were attributed to malicious gossip, but if Catharine and Robert Walpole did have a reconciliation that produced Horace, it was very brief. After the birth, they continued to lead their separate lives. Robert showed no interest in his fourth son who was not in the least like him, physically or mentally.

In these years between 1717 and 1720, Walpole and Townshend also helped establish something which was not to have a beneficial effect on British politics. That was the policy of deliberate mischief-making within the Whig party in pursuit of office. Bereft of power, they attacked Stanhope and Sunderland as heartily as did the Tories. These tactics were in future adopted by all disgruntled Whigs out of office. By the end of the eighteenth century, they had helped wreck the Whig party and were largely responsible for the long years which left Britain without an effective opposition, and thereby contributed to the Tory atrophy.

For Walpole and Townshend, ferociously attacking Stanhope and Sunderland was merely a tactical move which they hoped would dislodge the two noble lords from office. By 1719, it was obvious the tactics were not succeeding. Stanhope's record in foreign affairs had been brilliant. In 1714, England, as a result of Bolingbroke's management of the Treaty of Utrecht – however wise it might appear retrospectively – was without a friend in Europe. There was the danger of a full-scale war in the Baltic, the threat of a renewed war in the Mediterranean, while the traditional enmity between France and England more than simmered. Stanhope averted the full-scale northern war, settled the Mediterranean dispute and above all forged the alliance with France that gave Europe twenty years of stability. In the process, he continued the trend begun by Marlborough's victories, further establishing England as a leading European state, the country that could hold the balance of power.

Occupied with diplomacy, Stanhope mainly left home affairs to Sunderland who, under constant attack from Walpole and Townshend, did not succeed as brilliantly. However, the home record was far from disastrous, and both he and Stanhope retained the King's confidence. There was not the least sign that their ministry, however weak it might be on paper, was likely to fall. Apart from the fact that the tactics of Whig opposition to Whig were not succeeding, and that out of office he was growing short of money, Walpole was not a temperamental wrecker, nor was he a temperamental Tory. On the contrary, he genuinely believed in Whig tenets, that the Whigs were the people who would best serve the country's interests. What he also believed, of course, was that he was the Whig who could best serve his country's interests. Consequently, he came to the conclusion, for reasons both national and personal, that a *rapprochement* with Sunderland and Stanhope must be effected. But how?

The key to the *rapprochement*, as to everything else, was the King. But George had never liked Walpole, so how was he, out of office, away from the Court, to obtain a modicum of the King's confidence? The idea of effecting a reconciliation between George and the Prince of Wales occurred to him. This, in principle, everybody agreed would be an excellent thing. The King and his heir in conflict was not to the advantage of the country, and the man who could effect the reconciliation would prove his undoubted worth and power potential. Adroitly, brilliantly, Walpole set about the very difficult task of reconciling the father and son who loathed each other.

He had Caroline of Anspach's backing for the reconciliation which meant in fact, if not in theory, that he had the Prince of Wales's consent. Then he had another surprising ally, the former Mademoiselle Schulenberg, latterly Duchess of Munster, by now Duchess of Kendal. (In 1719, Stanhope and Sunderland granted her the English title she so desperately wanted.) Mademoiselle Schulenberg, or the Duchess of Kendal as we must henceforth call her, might be the King's *maîtresse en titre* but this did not mean that she was the only influence on him. Madame Kielmansegge was considerably younger and brighter than she was. In the last few years Madame Kielmansegge had become very friendly with the Hanoverian ministers who still had the King's confidence, somewhat to the exclusion of the Duchess of Kendal.

Also by this time, Stanhope and Sunderland were at loggerheads with the Hanoverians who had helped them to power in 1717. The two English lords were determined to weaken the influence of the German faction – Bothmar, Bernstorff and Jean de Robethon – if they possibly could; the Duchess of Kendal also wanted to weaken this influence, to spite her rival, Madame Kielmansegge; while on their side the Hanoverians wanted to get rid of Stanhope and Sunderland, and were working to persuade the King to appoint new leading ministers who would be indebted to them. It was round the web of personal jealousies and desires that Walpole, with his acute understanding of human weakness, patiently worked.

The Hanoverians were not in favour of the reconciliation with the Prince of Wales, because they thought that the King was not. Therefore, if the reconciliation could be effected, the Hanoverian position would be weakened. If Stanhope and Sunderland stayed in office, it would likewise be weakened. As the Duchess of Kendal would benefit, she started to work on the King to persuade him that the reconciliation would be a good idea. If Walpole was the obvious architect of the reconciliation,

Stanhope and Sunderland would be forced to take him back into the ministry. Moreover, if the Hanoverians were aiming to destroy their ministry, Stanhope and Sunderland needed Walpole and Townshend's abilities and strength. Thus Stanhope and Sunderland came round to the idea of re-admitting the two Norfolk upstarts to the government.

However, the King himself still had to be convinced that reconciliation with his son was a good idea. Despite the rival Court at Leicester House with its potential dangers, despite the Duchess of Kendal's pleas, George did not give a damn whether he spoke to his son again or not. So, before the King, Walpole dangled the prospect of money, £600,000 of money. This was the amount of debt accumulated on the civil list which the King's ministers – and the King – wanted written off by Parliament. There was only one person who could persuade Parliament to write off such a large sum. That was the man who understood England's country gentlemen, who knew just how far he could push them, who reacted to Parliament's every whim and mood – Robert Walpole.

With the Duchess of Kendal and the Earls of Sunderland and Stanhope reacting from ambition, the King from greed and the Prince of Wales pushed by his wife, Walpole achieved the remarkable feat: in the spring of 1720, George received his son in private audience at St James's Palace. Lady Cowper, who, as lady-in-waiting to Caroline of Anspach, was present – along with many other attendants, for no royal audience was very private in those days – recorded the scene thus:

> The Prince ... saw the King in his closet. The Prince made him a short compliment, saying it had been a great grief to him to have been in his displeasure so long; that he was infinitely obliged to H.M. for his permission of waiting upon him, and that he hoped the rest of his life would be such as the King would never have cause to complain of. The King ... could not speak to be heard but by broken sentences, and said several times, *Votre conduite, votre conduite*. ...

Later, according to Lady Cowper, everything was different, 'nothing but kissing and wishing of joy; and in short, so different a face of things, nobody could conceive that so much joy should be after so many resolutions never to come to this'.

However, the next day, after the dissident Whigs headed by

'The King could not speak to be heard but by broken sentences'

157

DOMINE

IN TE

SPERAVI

Sarga Finissima de Inglaterra de la P. Nueva Fabrica

N.° Con Yards

RIO DE   S E C S &   LONDRES

Walpole and Townshend had returned to the Court, the scene was again different. According to Lady Cowper, 'they [the King and the Prince] spoke not to one another nor looked at one another all the time, which caused many speculations. When the King came out, the Prince stood by him. The King spoke to most people except the Prince; they two only looked grave and out of humour.' In truth, grave and out of humour with each other, the King and his son remained for the rest of their lives together. Despite the speculations that the reconciliation would prove short-lived, and Walpole thrust back into the wilderness, the fragile harmony between the two Georges was not again broken. Walpole returned to office as Paymaster-General, and Townshend as President of the Council and Comptroller of the Household, both highly lucrative if not the most powerful of offices.

How long a ministry that included Stanhope, Sunderland, Walpole and Townshend, all jockeying for power, would have remained in united harmony is a matter for conjecture. As it was, only shortly after the Whigs became re-united, the South Sea Bubble burst. As all incidents of history, the roots of the South Sea Bubble lay way back. By the end of the seventeenth century, wars were lasting longer and costing more. Long or short term credit became an essential ingredient in the country's ability to wage war. Few understood this new financial weapon, credit, and speculation was rife. It was in an effort to give a more solid base to credit, to deal with the mounting national debt and the difficulties of transferring money to Europe for the various wars, that the Bank of England was founded in 1694.

The group of men in the City who founded the Bank of England were Whigs. As suppliers and raisers of money, the Bank's directors obviously became a powerful factor in politics, but they remained a Whig factor (and their support undoubtedly helped the Hanoverians to the throne). It was thus that, in 1711, prompted by political considerations, Robert Harley, soon to be Earl of Oxford, agreed to the foundation of the South Sea Company. It would take over £9,000,000 of the national debt in return for a monopoly of trade to South America. It would also provide a Tory counter-balance to the Whig-orientated Bank of England. It was from the trade monopoly with South America that the new enterprise took its name of the South Sea

The trade card of the South Sea Company, now in the Guildhall Museum.

159

Company. In fact, the company did very little trading in the south seas or anywhere else. Essentially it was a finance company set up to rival the Bank of England. By 1717, it was showing every sign of succeeding in its aim. It had become an established part of the credit system of the country, and its directors began to have grandiose ideas about further expansion. They were encouraged in the belief that England's credit resources were being sadly neglected by what was happening in France.

There, in 1716, a Scotsman called John Law had founded a bank and acquired the whole of the vast French national debt in return for a monopoly of foreign trade. On the strength of the monopoly, he circulated paper money and the effect was, apparently, sheer magic. From the depths of economic depression, France had soared into inflationary prosperity, and in 1718 the French Regent allowed Law's bank to become a national one. Then, in 1719, Law founded a trading company and everybody fought to buy shares in what would undoubtedly prove to be an equally fantastic success (it collapsed in 1720).

If Law could do this in France, surely somebody could do even better in England? England's economy was in a much more buoyant condition than the French had been. The directors of the South Sea Company realised that they would need government backing if they were to expand on the credit boom. They were a Tory-orientated organisation, and the government of the day was Whig. However, that worried neither them nor the King's ministers when the South Sea Company came up with the startling scheme to take over the whole of the national debt, then standing at £51,000,000, on terms highly advantageous to the government. Eventually, after intervention by the Bank of England supported by Walpole, early in 1720 agreement was reached for the South Sea Company to take over £30,000,000 of the national debt. The company expected to pay off the debt and make itself a profit, partly from the increased trading but mainly from the government confidence which would increase the value of its shares.

Once the deal was through Parliament, the shares did not just increase, they soared to astronomical proportions, helped by large bribes to encourage ministers, both British and Hanoverian, to buy shares. Within the blink of an eyelid, nearly

ABOVE The Prince of
Wales, later to become
George II. Before their
quarrel, he acted as his
father's interpreter at
Cabinet meetings, though
in many respects sharing
the elder George's Guelph
characteristics.
RIGHT Caroline of
Anspach, wife of the
Prince of Wales,
quickwitted and hungry
for power. Her close
friendship with Walpole
helped to bridge the gulf
between George I
and his son.

everybody in the country who had any money, however little it might be, was rushing to buy stock. The shares were not only in the South Sea Company. Each day, as the early summer months of 1720 rolled by, in the wake of the remarkable success of the government-approved South Sea Company, small companies shot up like mushrooms in the early morning. Many of them were for projects as ill-founded as the speculative madness that gripped the country. A few examples will show the span of this collective mania; into what the solid, sensible citizens of Great Britain were willing to put their life savings in the hope of a quick, large profit. Companies floated during the early summer months of 1720 included those –

> For supplying the town of Deal with fresh water.
> For the planting of mulberry trees and breeding of silkworms in Chelsea Park.
> For importing a large number of jackasses from Spain in order to propagate a larger breed of mules.
> For trading in human hair.
> For furnishing funerals to any part of Great Britain.
> For improving the art of soap-making.
> For a wheel for perpetual motion.
> For insuring of horses.
> For making oil from sunflower seeds.
> For the supply of all kinds of grass seeds and the changing of seed-corn.
> For assuring and increasing children's fortunes.
> For improving the land in the county of Flint.
> For wrecks to be fished off the Irish coast.
> For draining bogs in Ireland.
> For carrying on an undertaking of great advantage; but nobody to know what it is.

After some hundred-odd of such companies had been floated, the Government began to be alarmed. It passed the Bubble Act, which threatened legal action against any company operating without a proper charter. This stopped further small companies being formed but it did not halt the speculative mania. In mid-August, the first signs of panic were evident, when the South Sea Company applied for writs against four other companies. The intention was to prove that they were a solid, reliable, legal company whereas the other four were not, and that it was into the South Sea Company that the public should put its money.

The effect was to cause a decline in public confidence in all the companies, including the South Sea. By the end of August, share prices had dropped, and they went plumetting downwards and downwards throughout September until the market finally collapsed.

Financial ruin stared thousands of people in the face. One man wrote, 'You can't suppose the numbers of familys undone', and again, 'Those Devils of Directors have ruin'd more men's fortunes in this world, than I hope old Beelzebub will do souls for ye next', and finally but justly, 'The Directors have brought themselves into Bankruptcy for being cunning artfull knaves, I am come into the same State for being a very silly fool.' Why so many normally sensible citizens were such silly fools is difficult to assess. Greed obviously played a large part. Hysteria is a disease both contagious and infectious, but the widespread gambling instinct played its part, too.

There were a few people who read the financial omens correctly. Jonathan Swift wrote a poem which asked:

> Ye wise Philosophers! Explain,
> What Magick makes our Money rise,
> When dropt into the *Southern* Main;
> Or do these Jugglers cheat our Eyes?

And it predicted:

> The Nation then too late will find,
> Computing all their Cost and Trouble,
> Directors Promises but Wind,
> South-sea at best a mighty Bubble.

Sarah, Duchess of Marlborough was convinced 'that this project must burst in a little while and fall to nothing'. Wisely she kept her money in the Bank of England. Thomas Guy, said to be one of the meanest men in the country, managed to make a profit, a very handsome one too, nearly £20,000, by selling his shares at the right moment. It was with these vast profits that he founded Guy's Hospital in London, so some good came from the speculative mania. Horace Walpole later came up with the idea that the South Sea Bubble helped solidify the Hanoverian dynasty, 'by diverting the national attention from the game of Faction to the delirium of Stockjobbing'.

The 'game of Faction' was not over. The myth was later fostered that Horace's father, Robert Walpole, was among

'Those Devils of Directors'

those who recognised the basic unsoundness of the South Sea scheme from the start. He did not in fact do so. It was more by good luck than by brilliant foresight that Walpole emerged fairly unscathed financially – he had invested in the company – and more importantly, as the man who had not been politically implicated in the affair. That most of the King's ministers had been deeply involved in the South Sea Bubble was obviously true. Even if they had not been, the ruined and disillusioned citizens of the country wanted somebody's blood. Further, they wanted someone untainted by the scandal to impose order on the sudden chaos.

For a variety of reasons that person proved to be Robert Walpole. He was a Whig and therefore a member of the party that retained power, however grave the present crisis and wide-spread the hunt for scapegoats. He was also a member of the Government, but had only been so for a short time. Therefore, he was not directly associated with the disaster. He was known to have a sound grasp of financial matters and a high adminis-trative talent. Probably the action that focussed attention on Walpole as the one man who could rescue the country was unpremeditated on his part. For, at the height of the crisis, at the end of 1720, Walpole suddenly withdrew to his Norfolk home at Houghton.

He probably went because, having had the magnitude of the disaster spelled out to him, he felt that there was nothing he could do at this precise instance. Whether the withdrawal was prompted by acumen, instinct or the mood of the moment, it was a brilliant move. His physical absence from the panic and recriminations enveloping political London caused him to be mentally disassociated from the aftermath of the South Sea Bubble. There in Norfolk was Robert Walpole, a man of undoubted talent, perhaps genius; the man who had not involved himself in the mass hysteria and who therefore must have realised what the consequences would be; the man who was untouched by the stink of corruption that hung over other members of the Whig administration. The clamour to recall Walpole grew, and at the end of the year he returned to London to fight his last battles for supreme power. If his emergence as the man who could save his country from disaster was largely fortuitous, and based on a reputation for South Sea sagacity

Walpole at the peak of his power – he was the first 'Prime Minister', in the modern sense of the term.

The Crisis of the South Sea Bubble

The motive behind the foundation of the South Sea Company (as also that of the Bank of England in 1694) was to increase the credit of the country, an essential commodity if England were to wage war, especially as the national debt was rising rapidly. The Company took its name from a monopoly of trade in the South Seas market. The 'Bubble' burst when too many minor companies followed suit and the stock market collapsed, bringing financial ruin to many.

BELOW, RIGHT and BELOW RIGHT These contemporary cartoons show the impact the disaster – referred to in one as the 'incredible folly' – made on the nation. In

fact, the public's loss of
faith in the Government
and Establishment at this
time led to an increase in
popular pamphleteering
and the true beginnings of
political cartooning.

which he had not earned, once cast for the role Walpole proved himself to be more than equal to filling it.

Before leaving these turbulent years and following the Norfolk squire's route to supreme power, we must briefly return to the artistic scene. At least three notable works of art were produced in this period. 1717 saw the first performance of Handel's *Water Music*. One of Handel's biographers said that the suite was produced in 1715, as a peace-offering to George to placate the anger at his *Kappelmeister*'s prolonged stay in London. It is a nice story which has not been absolutely disproven, but diligent research by a German authority on the Hanoverians makes it seem more probable that the suite was produced in 1717. The *Water Music* was composed for a fête on the Thames, which is a pleasant thought, its majestic melodious strains floating across the dark, illuminated waters of London's river.

It was in 1719, as the South Sea Bubble was having air pumped into it, that Daniel Defoe's *The Life and Strange Adventures of Robinson Crusoe, of York, Mariner* etcetera (titles were very long in those days) was first published. Although the genesis of the

OPPOSITE Thomas Guy, noted for his miserliness, made a profit of nearly £20,000 when he sold his shares in the nick of time. BELOW The hospital which bears his name – one benefit which did accrue to the nation from his speculations.

The Satire of Swift and Defoe

The first half of the eighteenth century was a period when satire became the predominant form of literature. Joseph Addison, first editor of the *Spectator*, Sir Richard Steele and Alexander Pope achieved recognition only decades after their time, and it was the works of Jonathan Swift and Daniel Defoe which gained immediate success and have also stood the test of time.

DANIEL DE FOE.

TOP LEFT and BOTTOM LEFT
Two illustrations from an
early edition of *Robinson
Crusoe*.
FAR LEFT Daniel Defoe,
author of this first great
English novel.

ABOVE Jonathan Swift, the
genius whose satire often
bordered on the savage,
painted here by C. Jervas.
ABOVE and BELOW RIGHT
Gulliver's Travels: some
engravings in an early edition.

novel was already in being, *Robinson Crusoe* can justifiably be called the first great English novel. It was an immediate success, which was gratifying for the sixty-one-year-old Defoe who had been journalist and pamphleteer, and had had half a dozen other occupations in a life packed with vicissitudes. With its strong narrative line, its simple biblical language, its vivid attention to detail, *Robinson Crusoe* has continued to enthral generations of readers. It was the sense of reality, the conviction Defoe brought to a fictional tale based on fact (Alexander Selkirk's advantures in the West Indies in 1711) that most influenced the future shape of the English novel.

Appropriately, it was in 1720, as the South Sea hysteria burst, that Jonathan Swift first published *Gulliver's Travels*. This is one of the greatest works of satire in any language, penned by a man who can accurately be described by that over-used word, genius. *Gulliver's Travels* contains all of Swift's love of man and hatred of humanity, his consuming passion to cleanse the world by holding its lusts, its greeds, its pettiness, its ambitions up to ridicule, his corrosive wit and his lucid, vigorous prose. For those who did not and do not wish to see their images so savagely reflected, it was and is a first-rate entertainment. Swift himself said of the reflection, 'Satire is a sort of glass, wherein beholders do generally discover everybody's face but their own.' He also said, 'the chief end I propose to myself in all my labours is to vex the world rather than divert it'. This aim had its ill-effects on Swift's personal life, for the world as a whole does not want to be vexed. But as an artist he was wise enough to divert while he hopefully vexed some into reconsidering their attitudes.

We will leave the tortured, Anglo-Irish genius of Jonathan Swift with his mocking, affectionate comment upon his Anglo-German contemporary, George Frederick Handel, 'Ah, a German and a genius! a prodigy, admit him!'

RIGHT The Port of London: a painting by Samuel Scott showing the Old East India Wharf.
BELOW A collection of broadsheets and pamphlets issued at the time of the South Sea Bubble crisis.

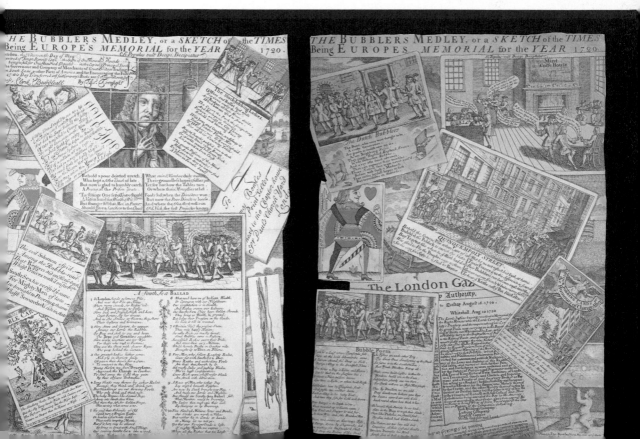

7 Sir Robert Walpole, Prime Minister 1721-6

GEORG.

THE KING WAS ONCE AGAIN in Hanover when the South Sea Bubble burst, though he returned to England with, for him, the minimum of delay after the situation had been explained by his ministers. George had also paid a visit to his beloved homeland in 1719, so he himself was not deeply associated with the scandal. But his mistresses, his Hanoverian entourage and his British ministers were. As most of the country viewed the matter, they had been involved solely for their own gain, knowing the affair to be financially hollow and riddled with corruption.

Walpole's problems, as he came to pick up the pieces at the end of 1720 and during the early months of 1721, were manifold. On the face of it, the King's ministers, who had indulged their greed and desire for private power rather than financial prudence and the country's interests, should go. The country at large certainly wanted heads to roll, and personally Walpole would not in the least have regretted the disgrace of Stanhope, Sunderland and their allies. But Stanhope and Sunderland were Whigs, and if the cry for retribution was met too heartily the Whig ministry would be destroyed and the Tories might be asked to form a new government. Nor could the Hanoverian ministers be allowed to emerge as scapegoats, because they were associated with the Whigs. Moreover, they were the King's friends and it was essential to retain George's trust.

Walpole's task was fraught with complications, and was by no means assisted by universal Whig backing. Another of the myths that later flourished was that Walpole returned from Norfolk, surveyed the mess and imposed order upon it; that this happened because he was the only man who could rescue his party and his country, and that the Whigs recognised these obvious facts. Some of them did no such thing. Old enmities and lusts for power died hard. Stanhope and Sunderland might be in a corner but they were seasoned politicians and bonny fighters. They did not allow Walpole an uninterrupted march to power over their inert bodies.

The first essential was to stabilise the financial situation and to restore some public confidence in the government's ability to manage the economy. It was Walpole who put forward a scheme to transfer South Sea Company stock to the Bank of England and the East India Company. In fact the scheme was

PREVIOUS PAGES A bust of Sir Robert Walpole, sculpted by J. M. Rysbrack.

OPPOSITE A portrait of George from the studio of Kneller.

177

devised by Walpole's junior minister and invaluable personal financial adviser, Robert Jacombe, and it was not put into practice. It was the banks themselves who eventually worked out their own salvation. But it was Walpole, by his grasp of essentials and his adroitness, who imposed a minimum stability in which the banks could find their own road to salvation. It was Walpole who manipulated a House of Commons thirsting for ministerial blood. In the process, he earned high public unpopularity – he was hooted by mobs – and the title of 'Skreen-Master General' (he officially remained Paymaster-General) because of the dexterity with which he defended – or screened – the reputations of the King's ministers.

It was a high political irony that Walpole had to defend the reputation and salvage the political future of his greatest enemy and rival, the Earl of Sunderland. But it was necessary because, if Sunderland were disgraced, the Whig ministry would inevitably fall. Sunderland retained the King's confidence, he had the ear of both royal mistresses and he wielded great patronage. More importantly, and Walpole sincerely believed this, it was necessary for the good of the country to bolster up the tainted Sunderland. A return to the Whig schisms of the last few years, or worse a return to the unstable Whig-Tory coalitions which had bedevilled Anne's reign, could perhaps lead to the disaster of rebellion. Alive and well in Italy was James Francis Edward, and the Stuarts could make great capital from a weak, strife-ridden administration in London.

Early in 1721, Walpole's other main rival, his erstwhile friend, Charles, Earl Stanhope, was decisively removed from the scene. He was not removed by any machinations of Walpole, but by sudden death. With Stanhope dead, Townshend was appointed Secretary of State in his place and the prospects of the Norfolk partnership were greatly improved. Then, in April 1721, Walpole himself received due recognition for his recent labours, being appointed Chancellor of the Exchequer and First Lord of the Treasury. But the salvaged Sunderland remained in office, and was not in the least grateful for vindication at Walpole's hands. On the contrary, in the way of human nature, the knowledge that he was indebted to Walpole made him hate the Norfolk squire more. It was widely recognised that dual leadership of the Whig party remained, the only difference being that the candidates had changed, Walpole and Townshend replacing Stanhope. But in 1721, few would have prophesied which candidate would emerge on top, and good odds could still have been obtained against Walpole. In truth, Sunderland had the edge, and his ability 'to remove from one office to another still retaining the character and influence of prime minister' was commented upon. Walpole himself, despite his basic fund of self-confidence and belief in his own abilities, was a prey to frequent anxieties about all manner of subjects. However smooth his road to supreme power may appear now, in 1721 Walpole knew that he still had a hard furrow to plough before he achieved it.

For a year, the battle raged behind the scenes between Walpole and Townshend and Sunderland, though they were careful not to make it too public, and too openly to split the Whig party. 1722 was the crucial year because it was an election

Antony House illustrates a home set in rambling countryside, typical of those of the landed gentry of the times.

John Carteret, later Earl Granville, Stanhope's protégé and a member of the Sunderland faction which threatened Walpole's pre-eminence.

year. Both sides wanted to preserve the Whig supremacy, but both wanted *their* Whig supporters to be returned so that the deadlock of dual power could be resolved. (Despite the splendid opportunity presented to the Tories by the South Sea Bubble, they remained too lacking in coherence to seize it and clinch an electoral victory.) Then, as the election results slowly started to come in, and everybody interested in politics held their breath to see whether the Walpole–Townshend partnership or Sunderland would emerge on top, 'the dull cold ear of Death' spoke to Sunderland.

Before it could be known whether Walpole–Townshend or Sunderland would be the victor, or whether the victory within the Whig party would be conclusive on either side, Sunderland was dead. This time there was only one man who could become the King's first minister, and that was the man who had so skilfully cleared up the South Sea Bubble mess. George still had

180

little liking for Robert Walpole but the Whigs had been returned to power, and in any case he favoured them. The day after Sunderland's sudden death, George summoned Walpole to St James's Palace. In fact, if not in name, he assumed the office of Prime Minister, the job he was to make so peculiarly his own and to retain for the next thirty years.

Walpole's road to the top was unquestionably smoothed by the sudden deaths of his two greatest rivals, Stanhope and Sunderland. What would have happened if Sunderland had not died so conveniently during the general election of 1722, is a fascinating question. With hindsight one can see that the moment Walpole definitely won his supreme power was in 1722, but it was still not at the time so apparent to the man himself. He lacked the King's confidence, and his mastery of the House of Commons was not paralleled by a similar mastery of the Court. Nor was his leadership yet undisputed within the Whig party. Stanhope's protégé, the young Carteret, threatened Walpole's supremacy, backed by the strength of the Sunderland faction. Much of the next two years were given over to further in-fighting between Walpole and Townshend and Carteret and the formidable Sunderland clique. Incidentally, Townshend still thought that he was his brother-in-law's political equal and social superior. To an extent, Walpole allowed this balance to remain. While he mainly devoted his talents to home affairs, Townshend spent his energies on foreign affairs. If not quite in the Stanhope class, Townshend proved an effective foreign minister, averting fresh threats of European warfare and further consolidating Britain's position as a leading power. The two men continued as a partnership, close friends and staunch political allies. It was only later, after the reign of George I, that Townshend, refusing to accept the fact of Walpole's pre-eminence, was forced into resignation.

One faction that went down with the South Sea wreck was that of the Hanoverians. Their reputations had been salvaged for political reasons, to protect the King, the Court and the involved Whigs. But, unlike the dead Sunderland, they were no longer a political necessity. On the contrary, British ministers were only too delighted to see the decline of their influence now that it had been proved – to a degree by Townshend, to a much greater extent by Stanhope and Sunderland – that the King's confidence could eventually be won without Germanic pressure. After the South Sea Bubble, neither Bothmar nor Bernstorff nor Jean de Robethon again exerted great power. This is not to say they were powerless, but their influence could now be circumvented.

In 1722, as Walpole, assisted by Townshend, moved towards the top, an event occurred which further smoothed his path to the undisputed summit. This was the uncovering of yet another Jacobite plot. It has been said that Walpole utilised Jacobite plots – real or imagined – skilfully and cynically to his own advantage, or at the very best to the Whig advantage. It has also been suggested that so astute a politician as Walpole knew full well that the Jacobite threat was hollow. But he did not recognise the hollowness – and twenty-three years later the Jacobite threat of Bonnie Prince Charlie was to be very real. The Stuarts had genuine support and Walpole was genuinely obsessed with the fear that they would again menace his country's stability and security.

However, it is true to say that Walpole made full political use of Jacobite plots. But he would have been a fool not to have done so, and nobody ever called Robert Walpole a fool (though he was called many pejorative things in his time). The Jacobites had been taken as much by surprise at the bursting of the South Sea Bubble as the majority of British citizens. They had failed to take advantage of that potential disaster. But they had decided that the 1722 elections would present them with an opportunity to strike on behalf of the Pretender. Their plans were as airy and disjointed as usual – there was an idea that the ubiquitous Duke of Ormonde might land in Kent – but there undeniably was a Jacobite plot. Its main conspirator was Bishop Atterbury of Rochester.

Atterbury was an intelligent, forceful character but he had a sad lack of judgment and an aggressive strain untempered by tact. He was an outspoken High Tory and a known Jacobite sympathiser. Previously, his silencing or arrest by the Whigs had been a difficult matter because his fearless, virulent attacks on them had earned him the admiration of all discontented sectors of the population. But in May 1722, news of a fresh Jacobite conspiracy was broken to the country, and Walpole skilfully built up the tension for the moment when the popular

Bishop Atterbury of Rochester, the leading force behind a Jacobite conspiracy. His arrest by Walpole greatly strengthen the esteem in which the minister was held throughout the country.

Atterbury would be arrested. The King's latest visit to Hanover was cancelled. The news was circulated that a threat had been made to assassinate him on the way to Hanover – anonymously and fortuitously revealed to the Duchess of Kendal. Thousands of troops were marched into Hyde Park, Catholics were ordered from the city and later Habeas Corpus was suspended.

In the event, the evidence against Atterbury was insufficient to convict him of treason, but it was enough to have him banished. Only one of the incompetent conspirators arrested, a barrister named Layer, was actually executed. Although Walpole was accused in a few quarters of over-doing the suppression of the half-baked plot, his firm handling of the situation was generally applauded throughout the country. It unquestionably helped re-establish the Whigs after the South Sea disaster. It also helped establish the man himself – as a contemporary wrote, 'it contributed very much to fixing Mr Walpole's interest and power with the King and manifested fresh proof of his abilities and usefulness as a minister'.

Another storm, and a less fruitful one, that bedevilled Walpole at this time was the affair of 'Wood's halfpenny'. A couple of years earlier, the Duchess of Kendal had been granted the patent to provide Ireland with coins – all coinage then being part of the King's prerogative. With her usual greed, she had sold the patent to a coin manufacturer named Wood for a handsome profit. Wood proceeded to supply Ireland with new copper coins which in fact were very good value. Sir Isaac Newton, in his capacity as Master of the Mint, attested to their worth. The Irish refused to accept the valuation and said that they were being fobbed off with wooden coinage to feather an Englishman's nest. All the frustrations of a subordinate race rose up, and Dean Swift, temporarily back home in Dublin after failing to gain preferment in England, became the brilliant mouthpiece of the Irish anger and discontent. While in England, Carteret and the Sunderland faction thought that they could utilise the Irish furore to bring about the downfall of Walpole and Townshend.

By 1724, Walpole and Townshend had out-manœuvred Carteret, not in fact over the Irish discontent but in the field of foreign affairs. They had squeezed Carteret into a position of causing a breach in the harmonious relationship between the young Louis XV and George I. Carteret was dismissed from his office as Secretary of State and, with particular irony, given the job of Lord Lieutenant of Ireland. There he had to deal with the continuing uproar over Wood's halfpenny, the uproar he had helped stir. In this affair, the Irish won a victory, and the coinage was eventually withdrawn. But once actually in Ireland, Carteret deemed it advisable to back Walpole rather than the dissident Irish nobles, so that overall victory was not theirs.

The result of Carteret's demotion was supreme power for Walpole. In two years, he had broken the Sunderland faction, secured the King's confidence, mastered the Court and demonstrated an unparalleled control of the House of Commons. He was in an unassailable position – not since Tudor times had one man held such power, as was noted in a contemporary rhyme:

> Such is the great Parallel as here behold,
> Walpole is now, what Burleigh was of old.

The next few years were among the sweetest of Walpole's life.

Undoubtedly Walpole wanted, and loved, supreme power. But then so did all his rivals who would have loved it just as much had they ever attained it. Walpole was not an idealist – he described himself as No saint, No spartan, No reformer. Nor was he a political visionary. He did not consciously set out to impose fresh limitations on the power of the King, to enlarge ministerial responsibility, to widen the role of Parliament or even to create the post of Prime Minister. Those things happened along the road. But if he was not a visionary, Walpole had some ideals. He believed fervently that war was a disaster, that problems could be solved by negotiation, that what his country needed was peace and prosperity. At any time, these are not bad beliefs. In the early eighteenth century, when the glory of battle had so long held the arena, they had a novel ring.

In pursuit of his beliefs and aims, Walpole worked from a typically practical basis at home, reorganising the fiscal system and the basis of the economy. He was again compared with a Tudor, and called England's greatest financial minister since Thomas Cromwell. Less usefully, he developed the existing concept of bribery and corruption as essential parts of the power structure to an outstanding degree. It must of course be remembered that nobody was paid for serving his country, neither Members of Parliament nor any of the King's ministers, including the Prime Minister. Unless a politician had a vast private income, he needed to recuperate or supplement the capital expended in his country's service. Thus, to a degree, the bribery and corruption were inherent in the system, and hence the rush to obtain the lucrative posts in the King's household and civil service. Deliberately, ruthlessly, Walpole set out to fill every possible office and place with people who owed him allegiance. What was unique about his efforts was that he bribed and

Walpole's prized salver, which he had made from the great seal of George I which was given to him as Treasurer. On it are engravings of London, Atlas and Justice which were designed by Hogarth. The silversmith was Paul de Lamerie.

corrupted with an efficiency that nobody had achieved before.

In the early years of his supreme power, Walpole brought peace and prosperity to his country. He was able to do this for the very reason that he held such supreme power. Initially, the effects were beneficial, because Robert Walpole was the man he was, possessed of a sort of vision, with the political and administrative genius to implement it, and because he was not a true despot. He believed in Parliament. Later, as he grew older and more tired, absolute power corrupted, not quite absolutely, but more than sufficiently to tarnish the vision. Offices, both major and minor, became filled with men who had nothing to give but their allegiance to Walpole. In other lesser hands the tight control of patronage he had instituted became a welter of bribery and corruption which eventually spelled disaster for the Whigs, and spread a rot through the whole country.

Walpole was not in his day noted for his patriotism, as he was not associated with any notion that had a high-sounding ring. It was Bolingbroke who was to the fore in developing the concept of patriotism in England, the concept of owing a wider, greater, nobler allegiance to the state rather than, as previously, to an individual lord or king. It was in the eighteenth century that the symbols of nationalism-cum-patriotism began to emerge. In England the symbol was John Bull – honest, reliable, dogged, fair-minded, peaceful by nature, aggressive if pushed, not over intellectual but streaked with surprising romanticism. Robert Walpole, the Norfolk squire who was anything but the average citizen, who derided such concepts as patriotism, became the symbol of the average Englishman. This is not perhaps as ironical as it might seem—Walpole wanted peace and prosperity because, in his own way, he loved his country.

During the years in which he first scented and then achieved his great power, Walpole had another pre-occupation, and that was the re-building of Houghton Hall, his ancestral home in Norfolk. When one considers that Walpole was frequently plagued with ill-health, his energy and achievements are doubly amazing. It was in 1720 that he decided to pull down the old rambling hall at Houghton and build a more fitting residence in its place. This decision, taken at such a time, underlines Walpole's ebullient optimism, because he could not see a clear road to power – and the attendant money necessary to build the fitting residence – in 1720. The pulling down of the old house and the construction of a temporary home took two years. It was appropriately in 1722, as Sunderland died and cleared the road to power, that the first stone of the new hall was laid. The entire building was not completed until the 1730s but it was habitable by 1726. By this date Walpole had solidified his position and though the original design had been grand, he proceeded to elaborate upon it.

Houghton Hall, the home
of the Walpole family to
which Sir Robert devoted
much time and money,
carrying out extensive
reconstructions and filling
the house with art treasures
collected from all over
Europe.

'Blown up by
gunpowder after
£200 a year
had been offered
to anyone who
could live there'

Houghton had not the vast, perfectly proportioned but extremely uncomfortable grandeur of Sir John Vanbrugh's country mansions, Blenheim or Castle Howard – or Eastbury in Dorset which was later 'blown up by gunpowder after £200 a year had been offered to anyone who could live there, and there were no replies'. Houghton was built as a house to be lived in. Although by modern standards it is massive and grandiose, for contemporaries it was more remarkable for its comfort. Nonetheless, it was built as a present and future monument of Walpole's greatness. When contemporaries saw or heard about Houghton, they could realise what Walpole, the Norfolk squire, had achieved, as could future generations. Walpole had another reason for constructing his imposing new home: he wanted a fitting setting in which to display his art treasures. If Walpole was not an intellectual and had little love of literature, his knowledge and love of art was wide and genuine. He was frequently lampooned as the philistine personification of John Bull, but he was in fact a great collector. Over the years, he built up a unique collection which included Titians, Rubens, Raphaels, Rembrandts and Poussins. Unfortunately it was sold by his profligate grandson to pay off debts. The country that benefited from Walpole's artistic taste and collecting instinct was not England but Russia. Catherine the Great bought the collection from the grandson who had inherited Walpole's talent for spending money without his ability to make it.

In 1725, Walpole flamboyantly demonstrated his power over the King by persuading George to resurrect the long-mouldering Knighthood of the Bath, and himself accepted a KCB. As a by-product of the restoration, Walpole had further patronage within his grasp – if it was the King who bestowed the resurrected honour, it was the King's trusted 'Prime Minister' who indicated where the honours should be bestowed. The following year, George, of his own volition, conferred upon Walpole the Order of the Garter. Walpole's delight knew no bounds, as he was one of the very few commoners ever to be thus honoured. He had the Star and the Garter worked into the design of the new ceilings at Houghton and he employed artists to paint the insignia on to his *old* portraits. His childish, fulsome delight in his honours earned him yet another nickname

190

– Sir Blue-String. However, one honour Walpole steadfastly refused to accept until the very end of his life, until he had retired, was elevation to the peerage. His refusal to become a noble lord is perhaps the best indication of how much he esteemed the House of Commons and was a Parliamentary man. Lord Chesterfield, among others, recognised this quality when he wrote of Sir Robert, 'He was both the best parliament-man, and the ablest manager of parliament, that I believe ever lived.'

Even during the first halcyon days of supreme power, Walpole's path was not entirely strewn with roses. Not everybody loved him or respected him, needed his patronage or thought that he was undeniably the only man who could lead the country. A strong opposition evolved, whose head, surprisingly, was Bolingbroke. The disgraced Tory leader, who had committed treason when he fled to France and joined the Pretender's service, was allowed to return to England in 1723. Despite the strong faction working for Bolingbroke's pardon, it was gracious of the Whigs to allow his return, particularly on Walpole's part, because he and Bolingbroke had been the most bitter enemies. Walpole's magnanimity was prompted partly by the general Whig lack of vengeance, partly by the certainty that he could keep Bolingbroke away from real power. Although Bolingbroke was allowed to reside in England again, his estates were withheld and he was barred from resuming his seat in the House of Lords. By 1725, the astute Bolingbroke had worked on the two royal mistresses and his estates were returned to him. (It was said that his wife paid the Duchess of Kendal an £11,000 bribe.) However, he did not succeed in getting the full pardon which would have allowed him to resume his seat in the Lords. Walpole saw to that, and very wisely from his point of view. Bolingbroke in unofficial opposition was one matter; Bolingbroke as a member of the House of Lords – whose power remained vast, however much Walpole himself esteemed the Commons – was another.

Into unofficial opposition Bolingbroke went. Dawley Farm, his rural retreat near Uxbridge, became the focus both for Tories and for malcontent Whigs. The latter followed the lead given by Walpole between 1717 and 1719, allying themselves with anybody who wanted the leader's downfall, providing Whig opposition to Whig. Bolingbroke quickly attracted back

The Flowering of Palladian Architecture

In 1715 Volume I of Colen Campbell's *Vitruvius Britannicus* brought to notice the designs of the Venetian architect Palladio. His ideas were embraced by the young Lord Burlington, who engaged Campbell to teach him the rudiments of architecture. With William Kent, they introduced the Palladian style which was to dominate the first half of the eighteenth century.

LEFT Houghton House: Campbell's first assignment, reminiscent of Inigo Jones's designs for Wilton House.
BELOW Chiswick House was designed by Burlington and building started in 1726. It is a copy of Palladio's Villa Rotonda, but finer than Mereworth.

RIGHT Mereworth Castle is Campbell's masterpiece. Completed in 1724, it was copied from Palladio's Villa Rotonda.

BELOW Wanstead House, also designed by Campbell, in Essex. Here he developed ideas introduced at Houghton.

the writers who had been his friends and allies in his days of power, Alexander Pope and Dean Swift, as well as John Gay who achieved immortality in the first year of George II's reign with *The Beggar's Opera*, and the young Henry Fielding who was to widen the horizons of the English novel.

In 1726, *The Craftsman* was launched by Bolingbroke and his friends. For the next ten years this magazine played a vital role in English politics, ceaselessly and mercilessly attacking Walpole and his administration. It attracted attention not only because of its venemous satire, which had all Europe laughing, but because of the quality of its prose and of its basically serious, at times high-minded political content. With such men as Bolingbroke lampooning him weekly and manœuvring against him daily, Walpole and his administration were not allowed to atrophy.

One example, probably written by Bolingbroke himself, which appeared in *The Craftsman* early in 1727, will show how the magazine attacked Sir Robert Walpole, 'The Great Man'. This particular extract, like many others which appeared in the magazine, has all the delicacy of a sledge-hammer, but it could be clearly understood by the mass of the population. It described Walpole's appearance at Court thus:

> He threw himself forward into the room, in a bluff, ruffianly manner. A smile, or rather a sneer, sat on his countenance. His face was bronzed over with a glare of confidence. An arch malignity leered in his eye. Nothing was so extraordinary as the effect of this person's appearance. They no sooner saw him, but they all turned their faces from the canopy, and fell prostrate before him. He trod over their backs, without any ceremony, and marched directly up to the Throne. He opened his Purse of Gold which he took out in handfuls and scattered amongst the assembly. ... He threw more gold, and they were pacified.

'*He threw more gold, and they were pacified*'

Despite the virulent opposition, the 1720s saw the emergence of a new England and it was shaped by Sir Robert Walpole. But these years also witnessed the passing of men who had been to the forefront in the late seventeenth-century upsurge of English vitality. In 1723, Sir Christopher Wren, who had created a native English architecture, died, and was appropriately buried in his crowning glory, St Paul's Cathedral. In 1726, came the death of Sir John Vanbrugh, who had further expanded the native style.

Vanbrugh's talents were astonishing. He was as brilliant a dramatist as he was an architect and two of his plays, *The Relapse* and *The Provok'd Wife*, have taken their place among the immortal few.

1722 marked the death of the Duke of Marlborough, indubitably the best-known Englishman of his day, at the ripe old age of seventy-two. He was given a magnificent state funeral in Westminster Abbey. (After Sarah's death, at her wish, the body was removed and they were interred side by side at Blenheim.) Jonathan Swift wrote a typical elegy, of the type not liable to increase his popularity, which began:

> His Grace! impossible! what dead!
> Of old age, too, and in his bed!
> And could that Mighty Warrior fall?
> And so inglorious, after all!

and ended:

> Let pride be taught by this rebuke,
> How very mean a thing's a Duke;
> From all his ill-got honours flung;
> Turn'd to that dirt from whence he sprung.

Sarah outlived the Duke by twenty-odd years, and joined her formidable talents to the opposition of Bolingbroke. To her is granted the last word on her husband; when, after his death, a suitor asked her to marry him, she gave the famous reply, '... if you could lay the empire of the world at my feet, you should never share the heart and hand that once belonged to John, Duke of Marlborough!'

8
The Death
of the King
1727

TOWARDS THE END OF HIS REIGN, George had been accepted by his British subjects. The stories of overmuch Hanoverian influence and corruption had diminished – the corruption was now mostly home-grown. The Duchess of Kendal and the new Countess of Darlington (Madame Kielmansegge obtained her English title in 1722) still interfered as much as they possibly could in Court and political matters, but they were no match for Walpole in the full bloom of his talents and power. In foreign affairs, fears that Hanoverian interests would take precedence over British had proved groundless. Having to give consideration to a King whose prime concern was Hanover and whose grasp of foreign affairs consisted of what he thought was good for Hanover, affected British foreign policy and was to continue to do so under George II. But first Stanhope, then Townshend, later Walpole himself demonstrated that the Hanoverian interest could be successfully subordinated to the British, and that the King could be kept happy in the process.

One step taken by George towards the end of his reign pleased his British subjects – 'he paid the nation the compliment of taking openly an English mistress'. Her name was Ann Brett and she was the daughter of the Countess of Macclesfield, the sister of Richard Savage, the poet. She had jet black hair and was very dark-skinned, 'so much so that she might have been mistaken for a Spanish beauty'. Her position was subordinate to that of the two long-established ladies, the Duchess of Kendal and the Countess of Darlington, but the young Miss Brett had ideas of supplanting the older women and becoming George's *maîtresse en titre*. It was said that insolence was 'the chief characteristic of the new Sultana'. Whatever her nature may have been, the appointment of a true-born English lady to share George's bed was regarded as an indication that he had some taste and had acquired some interest in his kingdom.

If George's British subjects accepted him as a tolerable monarch, they never grew to love him. But then there was little to love about him and little that he did to encourage his subjects' affections. He might have paid them the dubious compliment of taking an English mistress, but he never paid them the compliment of learning their language. Eventually, after twelve years in the country, George could follow a conversation in English, as long as it was spoken clearly and not too many

long words were used; his own command of the language remained execrable. He was cold and aloof at Court. He lived in unregal fashion in two rooms of the vast St James's Palace, eating and sleeping in one, receiving guests and holding audiences in the other. He spent most evenings in the Duchess of Kendal's apartments, not doing anything scintillating or even titillating, but indulging in the pastime of cutting paper into patterns. He appeared in public as infrequently as possible – he made only one tour of the English provinces throughout his reign (although the state of the roads did not encourage anybody to travel widely). When he appeared in public, as at the opera which he did enjoy, he tended to slip in rather than to make the desired royal entrance, and to sit in a private box rather than the royal one. But George was at least a good patron to Handel, whose pension of £200, granted by Queen Anne, he increased by a further £200.

Another matter that infuriated his British subjects was his

ABOVE The King, shown with the Prince and Princess of Wales, who set up their own Court at Leicester House.
FOLLOWING PAGES St James's Palace, hardly appreciated by George, who confined himself to the use of two of its rooms only.

Science and Philosophy in George's Reign

The eighteenth century was one of the most fruitful in the areas of science and philosophy. In the previous century, scientists had pursued their experiments in defiance of the Church's criticisms; likewise intellectuals now felt free to pursue a rational line of thought. Sir Isaac Newton and Gottfried Wilhelm Leibnitz both produced great new discoveries in mathematics, notably Newton's theory of gravity and Leibnitz's rules of calculus. Voltaire's philosophical works earned him the reputation of being a cynic.

ABOVE Sir Isaac Newton, who died in the same year as George.

RIGHT Voltaire, the philosopher who so greatly admired Newton.
BELOW RIGHT Leibnitz, whose company the Electress Sophia enjoyed. She appointed him librarian at Hanover.
BELOW The house in which Leibnitz lived in Hanover. It was unfortunately destroyed during the Second World War.

persistent and prolonged visits to Hanover. George had been made King of England. What more could any man ask for? Having had this immense honour bestowed upon him, in England he should stay and not be constantly journeying backwards and forwards to a small north German state from which anybody should be glad to escape. The more politically-conscious of George's British subjects also said that his frequent, lengthy sojourns in Hanover – he went in 1716, 1719, 1720, 1723 and 1725 – did not encourage smooth government. This was true, because George insisted on retaining all his prerogatives while in Hanover, and refused to leave a Regency empowered to act in his absence. In a time of crisis such as the South Sea Bubble, his absence could have been a disaster, because Parliament could not be recalled until he returned. Even in calmer years, the to-ing and fro-ing of couriers between London and Hanover considerably delayed ministerial action. However, it was a situation which everybody, even Walpole, had to accept because nobody, not even Walpole, could keep George from the delights and comforts of his birthplace.

In the early months of 1727, Sir Isaac Newton died, in his eighty-sixth year. Shortly before his death, the absent-minded, untidy, generous, warm-hearted man said, 'I do not know what I may appear to the world but to myself I seem to have been only like a boy playing on the seashore, and diverting myself in now and then finding a smoother pebble or a prettier shell than ordinary, whilst the great ocean of truth lay all undiscovered before me.' To the world, it seemed that he had dredged more than most from the great ocean of undiscovered truth. Voltaire was among the vast congregation that filled Westminster Abbey to pay their last tributes to Newton, and Voltaire said, 'if all the geniuses of the universe assembled, he should lead the band'.

By 1727, George himself was entering his sixty-seventh year. This was then considered a very good age, though if one did escape or survive the perils of smallpox and other diseases and natural disasters, longevity was not as uncommon as all that, to wit the Duke of Marlborough's and Sir Isaac Newton's. George had been fortunate to be blessed with good health, and his mother, the Electress Sophia, had lived to be eighty-four years old. Everybody was obviously aware that George was ageing,

John Gay, who composed
The Beggar's Opera in 1728,
is here painted by Aikman.

and all politicians were paying extra attention to the Prince of
Wales. Although Walpole had secured Caroline of Anspach's
friendship, he was still not beloved by the Prince, who had never
forgiven the terms forced on him in 1720 when Walpole had
arranged the reconciliation with his father. The opposition had
high hopes that on George's death Walpole's supremacy would
be broken, and the new King would summon a new minister to
form a new administration. However, there appeared to be no
immediate fear of the present King's demise, and George was
already making arrangements for yet another visit to Hanover
in the early summer.

If legend is to be believed, George had intimations of approaching death. According to one of the many stories that flooded Europe about the Elector of Hanover and his wife, Sophia Dorothea – a story given credence by Horace Walpole – a French oracle had prophesied that George would not survive her by more than a year. And in November 1726, Sophia Dorothea had died at Ahlden Castle. She had spent thirty-two years as a prisoner, the larger part of her life because she was only twenty-eight when she was first incarcerated. But it was said that in the last long years without freedom, without choice, she acquired a serenity and peace of mind. The spirit of the impetuous, self-willed, romantic woman died many years before the body of Sophia Dorothea.

The story of George being such a superstitious man is suspect. Closer contemporaries than Horace Walpole, who was after all only ten years old when the King died, denied that he was superstitious. They said that he was too phlegmatic to believe in oracles and prophesies. Horace Walpole's further story that as the King embarked for Hanover he took leave of the Prince and Princess of Wales, with tears in his eyes, saying that he would never see them again, is even more suspect. The notion of George crying at the thought of never seeing his detested son again is hardly credible.

Before George embarked on what was indeed to prove his last journey to Hanover, he celebrated his sixty-seventh birthday. According to a contemporary newspaper, 'There was a numerous court at St James's to compliment his Majesty on that occasion. The Knights of the order of the Garter, Thistle and Bath appeared in their collars of SS and jewels; at noon the guns fired in the park and at the Tower; and the evening concluded with all possible demonstrations of joy throughout the cities of London and Westminster.' (The collar of 'SS' was a chain of gold whose links were shaped into the letter 'S'. It was a personal gift of the sovereign.) Also before the King's departure, it was noted in the newspaper, 'A council was held at Whitehall when the Regency was settled on the same foot as the last.' This meant that the Prince of Wales was left with as little power as possible, though with slightly more than on George's first visit to Hanover in 1716.

Two nights before George left England, Horace Walpole

Horace Walpole, who was only ten when he saw the aged King, who was to die a few days later.

was taken by his mother to see the King. Arrangements to get the ten-year-old child into the King's apartments were complicated, and effected only by the kind offices of the Duchess of Kendal. Presumably, in this instance, she worked without payment, as Horace would surely have mentioned a bribe had it been paid. The child was transfixed by the occasion and the honour, but his brain continued to work and he later wrote one of the best first-hand descriptions of George I: 'The person of the King is as perfect in my memory as if I saw him but yesterday. It was that of an elderly man, rather pale, and exactly like to his pictures and coins; not tall, of an aspect rather good and august, with a dark tye wig, a plain coat, waistcoat and breeches of snuff-coloured cloth, with stockings of the same colour, and a blue riband over all.' Of the Duchess of Kendal, who had arranged the audience, Horace merely noted that she was 'a very tall, lean, ill-favoured old lady'.

On 3 June 1727, George embarked for Hanover in the company of the ill-favoured old Duchess and a small entourage, which included his Turkish servant Mustapha. Townshend was also among the party, but he left the King in Holland and made his own way to Hanover, engaging in diplomatic affairs as he went along. Even had Walpole wished to accompany the King, he would not have been able to have done so. For much of May he had been 'extremely ill of a violent looseness', in his brother's words, and was only beginning to climb back to health. In fact, George himself had not been too well. Just before he was due to set off, he suffered from what were described as fits, but he appeared to have recovered from the attacks. It would have needed more than a few minor fits to have prevented George from embarking for the only place in which he felt truly contented and at home.

The North Sea crossing was successfully accomplished, and by 9 June George and his party were at the small town of Delden in Holland. They stayed there overnight and George consumed an enormous meal which included a vast quantity of melons – 'an act of imprudence to which was subsequently ascribed the disorder that caused his death'. On the morning of 10 June, having partaken only a cup of chocolate, the King left Delden. Mustapha was among the small party that accompanied him, but the Duchess of Kendal was not. For some reason she decided to stay in Delden and follow the King later. Only an hour's journey out of Delden George fainted but he recovered consciousness and insisted on continuing with the journey. There is some confusion as to where and at what point he actually died. Some versions have him dying as the coach rattled towards Osnabrück, but contemporary English newspapers ran the following version:

> Our most late Gracious Sovereign was seized with a sudden illness ... as he was in the coach between Delden and Nordhorn on his way to Hanover; his majesty was presently let blood, and had such remedies as were judged proper administered to him; and travelled on to his Highness the Duke of York's at Osnabruck, where he arrived about ten that night. But notwithstanding all the physicians could do for his recovery, he departed this life on the 11th. about one in the morning, in the 68th. year of his age and 13th. of his Reign; a Prince endowed with all the royal virtues.

Death was attributed to 'a fit of an apoplexy'. Apart from the story that the fit was brought on by severe indigestion caused by over-indulgence in the melons, there was another reason given for George's sudden death. This inevitably was connected with Sophia Dorothea. She was supposed to have written George a letter just before her death. In the letter she protested her innocence in the Königsmark affair and said that George had used her cruelly. As George left Delden, the letter was delivered into his hands, he duly started to read it in the coach and its contents were supposed to have brought on the apoplexy. Again it is an unlikely story. George had managed to ignore Sophia Dorothea for thirty years and had suffered no pangs of conscience about her during that period. The chance of his having a fit on reading a letter from her, even a death-bed affirmation of innocence, is not great.

News of the King's first fainting spell was conveyed to the Duchess of Kendal, who left Delden immediately on its receipt. By the time she reached Osnabrück, George was dead. It was said, 'she beat her breast, tore her hair' and somewhat anticlimactically 'gave signs of extreme fatigue'. At least one person apparently genuinely mourned the passing of the first Hanoverian King of England, as probably did the faithful Mustapha who was present when George died. Incidentally, there were also persistent rumours over the years that George had married

'She beat her breast, tore her hair and gave extreme signs of fatigue'

209

the Duchess of Kendal with his left hand, according to the Continental custom for kings and commoners. It was even said that the Archbishop of Canterbury had performed the ceremony, which again does not sound very likely, particularly as the Duchess was an ardent Lutheran.

The news of the King's death was conveyed to London as post-haste as possible. It arrived on 14 June, the messenger carrying it going straight to Sir Robert Walpole's Chelsea house. Fortunately, Sir Robert was at home and, as the late King's first minister, he drove out to Richmond Palace where the Prince and Princess of Wales were in residence. A master of the difficult art of farce could not have constructed a better scene than the one which ensued at Richmond. It was after dinner by the time that Walpole arrived at the Palace. The lusty Prince of Wales was already in bed with Caroline but this was one piece of news which could not wait until the morning. A lady of the bedchamber was ordered to request the Prince's immediate attendance on Sir Robert. Flustered and bad-tempered, only half-dressed and holding his breeches in his hand, the Prince emerged. He stared in astonishment as Walpole lowered his vast bulk to a kneeling position and broke the news of his father's death and his consequent assumption of the crown. George II's reported comment on being acquainted with these facts was, 'Dat is one big lie.' If it was true, it reveals the extent of his confusion, because the idea of Walpole riding out to Richmond, summoning the Prince from his bedchamber to inform him that he was King of England as a joke, is beyond the bounds of feasibility.

The King was dead! Long live the King! Also long live Sir Robert Walpole! The hopes of the opposition proved so much dust, though in the first inevitably confused days of the new reign, they rode high. The opening lines of 'an heroic poem' entitled *Robin's Pathetic Tale* demonstrates how the opposition saw the situation.

> Unhappy me amongst the Birds of Prey,
> Once I'd a comfort, now he's turned to clay

(Robert Walpole was frequently referred to as Robin, and the allusions to various predatory birds attacking not-so-helpless Robin were endless.) But 'pathetic Robin' managed not to be dismissed as the new King's first minister. Within a very short

The Tale of the Robbin,
and the Tom-titt,
Who all the Birds in
the Air have bitt.

See here o'er the Grid-Iron, the Mony they tell.
While Peices (like Taylors,) they Sink into H———l.

time, with the assistance of Caroline, he had won the monarch's liking and respect and he became more indispensable to George II than he had been to George I. However, that is another story.

The old King was dead but not yet buried. For several weeks the newspapers ran items announcing that his body would be brought from Hanover for burial in Westminster Abbey. In the event, George I was one of the few Kings of England buried outside the country, and all that happened in England was that the courtiers were ordered to 'put themselves in deepest mourning (long cloaks excepted), the said mourning to begin on Sunday the 25th. instant'. Duly, on 25 June, there was a 'vast appearance at court … The King appeared in purple, and the

A cartoon directed against Walpole, who was often nicknamed 'Robin' by the opposition to his Whig ministry.

Queen in black bombazine.' When it became apparent that the late King's body was not being brought back to London, there were further news items intimating that he had been privately interred in Hanover. In fact, it was not until the beginning of September that George was finally interred. But he was buried in his beloved Hanover, and the occasion caused little stir in England.

One or two newspapers covered the event thus:

> In the night between the 3rd. and 4th. instant, the corpse of our late King was delivered without ceremony, at Osnabruck, into the hands of the present King of Great Britain's officers, and conducted by a detachment of the Duke of York and Bishop of Osnabruck's Life Guards, who were there relieved by a detachment of the Regiment of the Dragoons of Wenden, which guarded the procession two nights; after it was escorted by a detachment of Dragoons of the Regiment of Pontius Pilate as far as the plain between the Ahle and Limmer, where 60 of our Life Guards received it at midnight and conducted it hither, the cavalcade arriving about one o'clock before the Gate of Callenberg.

The funeral procession entered the town, at its head two domestics on horseback, 'with each a lighted flambeau in his hand'. They were followed by a trumpeter on horseback, a coach containing the late King's surgeon and valets and a mounted escort 'with drawn swords, pointed backwards under the left arm'. Then came the coach bearing the King's coffin and his personal escort, two more trumpeters 'resting their trumpets bottom upward', pages, gentlemen of the Court, footmen with lighted candles and the burghers of Hanover also with lighted flambeaux. The procession entered the castle yard, and the coffin was lifted from the coach and borne by sixteen colonels to the vault. It was noted that the church and the quadrangles of the castle were 'all finely illuminated'; and 'notwithstanding the unreasonable time of night when the burial was performed, there was a great concourse of people from all parts to see, with tears in their eyes, this last honour paid to their late sovereign, once the joy and delight of his subjects'.

Having recovered from her grief, the Duchess of Kendal refused to believe that the old King was truly dead. Some time before his death, he was supposed to have told her that 'if it were possible for the departed to return to this world he would make

'There was a great concourse of people from all parts'

212

her a visit'. Accordingly, when a raven flew in through the window of the Duchess's villa at Isleworth, she was, as Horace Walpole maliciously recounted, 'persuaded it was the soul of her departed monarch so accoutred, and received and treated it with all the respect and tenderness of duty, till the royal bird or she took their last flight'. The vision of the long, emaciated, elderly Duchess of Kendal ministering to the needs of a raven as if it were the King is as farcical as the accession scene at Richmond Palace. The idea of taking the raven-King back to its beloved Hanover did not apparently strike her superstitious soul. Or perhaps, being kinder, she had grown to like England (she had become naturalised several years before). Certainly, England had proved extremely fruitful soil for her. It was rumoured that, in his Will, which was never officially revealed, George I left the Duchess of Kendal £40,000. She lived to enjoy it and the rest of the fortune accrued during her years of power until she was into her eighties.

George's death was obviously not the signal for mass mourning in England. As he was buried in Hanover, there was not even the opportunity for the citizens to show any respect they might have, or indulge their love of ceremony, in a state funeral. The panegyrics on George's reign did not pour forth, though there was a trickle, and Anne Brett's poet brother, Richard Savage, produced an ode to the memory of the late beloved monarch. There has never been a flood of literature about the first Hanoverian King. He remains one of the more under-written of England's monarchs. This was probably inevitable, because he was not of himself a fascinating or particularly interesting man. He was inarticulate and uncommunicative. He established no glittering Court. His mistresses were distinguished only by their ugliness, their limited brains and their rapacity. Consequently he has never captured the popular imagination. George was overwhelmed by the massive figure of Sir Robert Walpole. The interest of his reign lies in his being the first monarch ordained by Parliament, the internal struggles for power, the emergence of Walpole and the sowing of the seeds of Parliamentary monarchy.

Nonetheless, George contributed to the development of Parliament's power which led ultimately to the people's power – if, like the earlier Parliaments, they chose to exercise it. His

contribution was not based entirely on the negative facts of his dullness, indolence and lack of interest. Admittedly, as Lord Chesterfield later wrote, 'England was too big for him.' His narrow mind could grasp only the simplicity of a small despotic state such as Hanover. He never began to understand the reasons which had driven, and were driving, the English people towards a political maturity. But however large a part his laziness and lack of interest played in a vital development of government, George himself had sufficient good sense not to interfere too much. He accepted the strictures laid on him by the Act of Settlement. He accepted the advice of his ministers. And however clever Walpole was, George also had sufficient acumen to back him. Had the King not eventually recognised the Great Man's qualities, Walpole would not have gained his supreme power which allowed England to prosper and advance.

Indulging in the frowned-upon but nonetheless engrossing pastime of trying to re-route the course of history, what was the alternative to George? The return of the Stuarts? Suppose the Stuart supporters had been better organised and had achieved a successful rebellion: James III would have been crowned – probably he would have enjoyed the ceremony more than George and responded with greater enthusiasm to his subjects' cheers. But the possible James III believed in the Divine Right of Kings. Nothing in his character demonstrated an ability to select men of talent to serve him. Nor did he show any ability to accept political reality, to realise that compromise is an essential ingredient of life and one, moreover, on which his British subjects thrived. He was an ardent Catholic who believed that the true religion should be extended to all. Whether or not he had endeavoured to bring England back into the Catholic fold, the probable results of his reign would have been sectarian strife; an unholier scramble to gain the King's confidence than ensued with George, with second-rate men emerging on top and Walpole nowhere to be seen, because divinely appointed kings and Norfolk squires would not have mixed; a disintegration of the embryonic party system with its strong opposition; and an indefinite delay in the development of Parliament's power; in the end, probably, another civil war.

If this is an over-coloured view, based on rotten foundations

George I maintained an interest in hunting and horse-riding to the end of his life, as this fine equestrian portrait shows.

215

because nobody can know what would have happened if James Francis Edward had regained the throne, it does seem fairly safe to say – from the actual Stuart record – that stability was not an atmosphere that family engendered. For all his dullness, his laziness, his obstinacy, his less pleasant characteristics as exhibited towards his own family, his lack of glittering personality, George had sufficient intelligence not to overplay his hand. He had a sort of passive solidity which allowed Sir Robert Walpole to emerge and his adopted country to flourish.

When George died, Britain had a strong, stable government and was, relative to other European nations and to what she herself had been, a prosperous, contented country. The politicians and populace of Great Britain surely did well to back the House of Hanover rather than the House of Stuart.

A coronation medal made of an alloy of copper and tin known as 'speculum'. On it, George's name is represented in heraldic symbols.

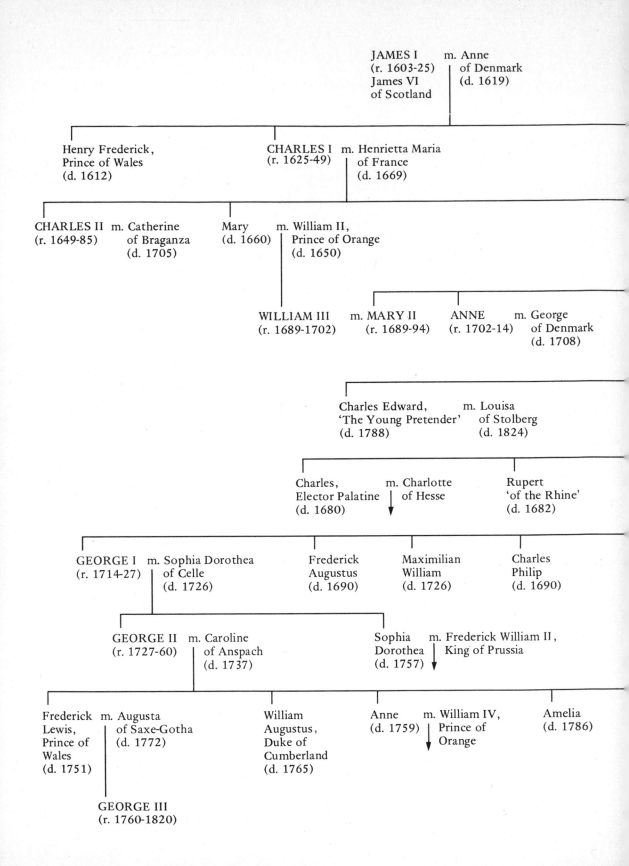

JAMES I
(r. 1603-25)
James VI
of Scotland
m. Anne
of Denmark
(d. 1619)

Henry Frederick,
Prince of Wales
(d. 1612)

CHARLES I
(r. 1625-49)
m. Henrietta Maria
of France
(d. 1669)

CHARLES II
(r. 1649-85)
m. Catherine
of Braganza
(d. 1705)

Mary
(d. 1660)
m. William II,
Prince of Orange
(d. 1650)

WILLIAM III
(r. 1689-1702)
m. MARY II
(r. 1689-94)

ANNE
(r. 1702-14)
m. George
of Denmark
(d. 1708)

Charles Edward,
'The Young Pretender'
(d. 1788)
m. Louisa
of Stolberg
(d. 1824)

Charles,
Elector Palatine
(d. 1680)
m. Charlotte
of Hesse

Rupert
'of the Rhine'
(d. 1682)

GEORGE I
(r. 1714-27)
m. Sophia Dorothea
of Celle
(d. 1726)

Frederick
Augustus
(d. 1690)

Maximilian
William
(d. 1726)

Charles
Philip
(d. 1690)

GEORGE II
(r. 1727-60)
m. Caroline
of Anspach
(d. 1737)

Sophia
Dorothea
(d. 1757)
m. Frederick William II,
King of Prussia

Frederick
Lewis,
Prince of
Wales
(d. 1751)
m. Augusta
of Saxe-Gotha
(d. 1772)

William
Augustus,
Duke of
Cumberland
(d. 1765)

Anne
(d. 1759)
m. William IV,
Prince of
Orange

Amelia
(d. 1786)

GEORGE III
(r. 1760-1820)

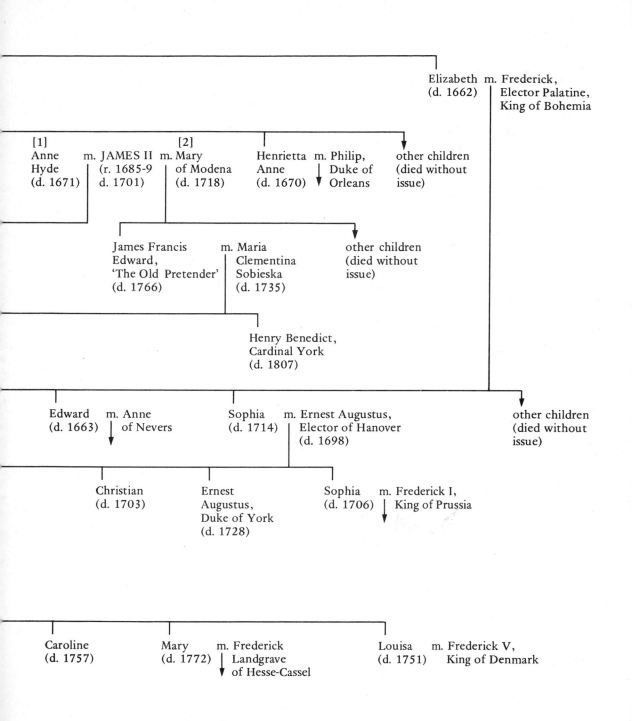

Elizabeth m. Frederick,
(d. 1662) | Elector Palatine,
King of Bohemia

[1]
Anne   m. JAMES II [2]
Hyde   (r. 1685-9   m. Mary   Henrietta m. Philip,   other children
(d. 1671) d. 1701)   of Modena   Anne   Duke of   (died without
                      (d. 1718)   (d. 1670) Orleans   issue)

James Francis   m. Maria   other children
Edward,   Clementina   (died without
'The Old Pretender' Sobieska   issue)
(d. 1766)   (d. 1735)

Henry Benedict,
Cardinal York
(d. 1807)

Edward   m. Anne   Sophia   m. Ernest Augustus,   other children
(d. 1663) | of Nevers   (d. 1714) | Elector of Hanover   (died without
                                    (d. 1698)   issue)

Christian   Ernest   Sophia   m. Frederick I,
(d. 1703)   Augustus,   (d. 1706) | King of Prussia
                Duke of York
                (d. 1728)

Caroline   Mary   m. Frederick   Louisa   m. Frederick V,
(d. 1757)   (d. 1772) | Landgrave   (d. 1751)   King of Denmark
                          | of Hesse-Cassel

Select bibliography

Baily, Francis E. *Sophia of Hanover and her Times* (1936)

Baynes, John. *The Jacobite Rising of 1715* (1970)

Brown, John. *Anecdotes and Characters of the House of Brunswick* (1821)

Churchill, Winston. *Marlborough, his Life and Times* (1947 edition)

Cowper, Lady. *Diary 1714–1720* (1864)

Coxe, William. *Memoirs of the Life and Administration of Sir Robert Walpole, Earl of Orford* (1798)

Doran, John. *London in the Jacobite Times* (1877)

Green, David. *Queen Anne* (1970)

Green, V. H. H. *The Hanoverians 1715–1815* (1948)

Greenwood, A.D. *Lives of the Hanoverian Queens of England* (1909)

Hardwicke, Earl of. *Walpoliana* (1781)

Jesse, John Heneage. *Memoirs of the Court of England from .. 1688 .. to George II* (1843)

Leadham, I.S. *A Political History of England 1702–1760* (1921)

McInnes, Angus. *Robert Harley, Puritan and Politician* (1970)

Melville, Lewis. *The First George* (1908)

   The South Sea Bubble (1921)

Michael, Wolfgang. *The Beginnings of the Hanoverian Dynasty* .(English translation 1936)

Morley, John. *Walpole* (1889)

Petrie, Sir Charles. *Bolingbroke* (1937)

Plumb, J.H. *Sir Robert Walpole – The Making of a Statesman* (1956)

   The King's Minister (1960)

   The First Four Georges (1956)

Rait, Robert S. *Five Stuart Princesses* (1902)

Robertson, C.Grant. *England under the Hanoverians* (1912)

Sichel, Walter. *Bolingbroke and his Times* (1901)

Sinclair-Stevenson, Christopher. *Inglorious Rebellion* (1971)

Tayler, A. and H. *The Story of the Rising* (1936)

Thackeray, William Makepeace. *The Four Georges* (1861)

Toland, John. *An Account of the Courts of Prussia and Hanover* (1705)

Trevelyan, G.M. *England under Queen Anne*

   Blenheim (1930)

   Ramillies and the Union with Scotland (1932)

   The Peace and the Protestant Succession (1934)

Walpole, Horace. *Reminiscences* (1924 edition)

Ward, Sir A. W. *Great Britain and Hanover* (1899)
    The Electress Sophia and the Hanoverian Succession (1903)

Wilkins, W. H. *The Love of an Uncrowned Queen* (1900)

Williams, Basil. *The Whig Supremacy 1714–1760* (1962 edition)
    Stanhope (1932)

Wortley Montagu, Lady Mary. *Letters and Works* (1861)

Wright, Thomas. *England under the House of Hanover* (1848)

Index